Comrade in Arms

Comrade in Arms

Dibyendu Palit

Translated from the Bengali
'Sahajoddha'
by
Sahana Ghosh

Rupa & Co

Text Copyright © Dibyendu Palit 2004

Translation Copyright © Sahana Ghosh 2004

Published by
Rupa & Co
7/16, Ansari Road, Daryaganj,
New Delhi 110 002

Sales Centres:
Allahabad Bangalore Chandigarh
Chennai Hyderabad Jaipur Kathmandu
Kolkata Ludhiana Mumbai Pune

All rights reserved.
No part of this publication may be reproduced, stored in a
retrieval system, or transmitted, in any form or by any means,
electronic, mechanical, photocopying, recording or otherwise,
without the prior permission of the publishers.

Typeset in CG Times by
Excel Publishing Services
138/B, Munirka, New Delhi 110067

Printed in India by
Gopsons Papers Ltd
A-14, Sector 60,
Noida-201 301

Chapter 1

He doesn't have to wait even ten seconds after walking out of the lift and pressing the calling bell. The door opens immediately.

A while ago, with no sign of the watchman at the gate, Aditya had asked the taxi driver to blow the horn. From the road he noticed the watchman approaching and the flat lighting up. It's a quarter to three now. Difficult to make out whether it's day or night. At this time, men are in deep slumber, thieves are busy in action. The street lights seem superfluous—rather the darkness and silence grows thicker.

The lights turned on so promptly implies that Mahasweta is awake.

Poor thing! She's so fond of sleeping. If there's no party or some urgent work, she hurries for dinner at nine; her day ends at ten, ten-thirty. Her night's sleep has been spoilt today, having to keep awake till so late. If she goes to bed now, even if she sleeps late she'll be drowsy all day tomorrow.

But it's not Mahasweta who opens the door.

Pritha. Her features resemble her mother's, except that her complexion is a little darker, inherited from Aditya. The slightly thick lips are the same as his.

Aditya says, "You too are up!"

"Not me too. Only me." Pritha takes the twenty-four inch suitcase from Aditya and says, "You really got me worried!"

"I know!" Aditya has already walked to the middle of the living room. He asks, "Where's your mother?"

"Not home—"

"Why!"

"Dadu's heart has been giving trouble from the morning. She's there."

"Then?"

"She called at eleven. He's okay. They've taken off the oxygen. Abdul wasn't back yet. I told her to stay back. It was raining badly too."

Aditya sits on the sofa and unlacing his shoes, says, "Did Abdul go to the airport?"

"He was waiting there from seven." Pritha switches on the fan before sitting across him. Then she says, "At around nine he said the plane was two hours late. A little later he called again and said there was no news of the Bombay flight—it might not arrive if the weather didn't improve. He asked if he should wait. I told him to come back—"

Aditya glances up at his daughter. She's wearing a sky blue nightie. Bare neck, no ear ring. Thick tresses of hair falling down her shoulders almost to the waist. It's not enough to say she's pretty; her features are almost perfect. Pritha's brow, eyes, nose and chin demand something more than appreciation. If she was perfectly fair, her brightness would have been subdued by her charm. The forty seven year old, Aditya sometimes feels that Pritha compensates to a great extent what Sweta lacks. The serenity on her face pleases him. He says, "You've done the right thing. He would have been stuck there for four hours unnecessarily."

"Was it a lot of trouble coming?"

Although his earlier words were meant to console her, Pritha still sounds guilty for asking the driver back.

Aditya smiles as he pulls off his shoes.

"What trouble! Took the airlines bus up to Grand Hotel. Then taxi—"

"You got a taxi?"

"I did. But of course, it took many attempts and a double fare. Not only extra fare, they refused to budge an inch unless they got more than one passenger. The rate at which murders are happening all around."

Even at the disturbing words, a smile spreads across Aditya's face. As if it reminds him of something.

Pritha's brow creases in surprise.

"What are you smiling at?"

"When one taxi after another refused, an old Sardarji came forward. He said, come on, let's die together. We may be slaughtered at Wood Street, if not at Dum Dum. On the way, he said, one can risk one's life for extra fare—as if a taxi ride itself is a risk, someone or some people waiting inside to kill."

The story doesn't have much sting. Not enough substance to shake Aditya, to amuse him. He is a man of few words. Yet Pritha is relieved. If you are relaxed you can pay heed to irrelevant things as these. Not just that, the plane journey doesn't seem to have tired Aditya.

"It's not very amusing, Baba." Pritha says, "You haven't seen today's papers. Day before yesterday, early in the morning, four boys were shot dead at Beleghata canalside."

"I know." Aditya sounds normal. He looks away from Pritha towards the balcony, and mutters, "Two gentlemen were talking about it in the bus. Apparently, a lot of people were woken up by the sound of bullets, many eye witnesses. A lady recognised two of the boys from her window—local boys. They threw sand over the blood and carried the bodies in the van—"

As he concludes, Aditya shakes his head in disgust and disbelief. He clenches his fist and taps his knees, bites his lower lip. His eyes become unusually keen and slanted.

Some big vehicle is clattering down the street. Maybe a lorry or a van. Another one follows in a minute. But the second noise is only that of speed. It seems to follow the previous one, maybe it's in pursuit. At the start of the noise, one or two disturbed dogs bark in annoyance. As the sound of the vehicles fade away, more start barking. In the midst of this cacophony, another vehicle runs over one of the dogs and speeds away in the same direction. A bark gets distorted in a nasty way—no reason not to recognise the cry. It would possibly seem like that of a jackal's, if you heard it all of a sudden. Gradually the wails and cries calm down. A crow emerges from the mango tree across the street, flies in the air for a while, takes a bend and disappears behind the tree.

Aditya remains silent for some time and then rises, shoes in hand.

"Where's Bacchu? Sleeping?"

"What else?" Pritha hides her feelings for her father's sake and says, "We played ludo till midnight. He couldn't keep awake after that—"

"Midnight! That's a torture." He looks at her daughter with indulgence and says, "That's very courageous of you."

"Not really." Pritha says, "Ma wasn't home. I didn't know whether you would be back. I even thought of calling Satya from his quarters—"

"Good you didn't . It's normal to feel scared, but you were inside the flat. There's no dearth of protection here—"

Two of the three bedrooms are usually so used. One for the husband and wife and one for Pritha-Bacchu. The third room has been converted into a study. Aditya reads and writes here. It's become such a habit that he can't concentrate unless he sits on his own desk; he feels lost otherwise. When he's not home, or when he goes on tour, Pritha uses the room. The girl is quite serious about her studies. She's doing her B.A. in English honours, final year. She should have a room of her own now. If not for the same reason, Sweta too wants Pritha and Bacchu to have separate rooms—Bachchu is growing up. His twelfth birthday has just got over.

Aditya peeps through their bedroom curtains and sees his son sleeping. He stands still. He had heard everything with his ears pricked. Sixteen to thirty-six—any male of this age group is a target. And then shooting them! If Pritha was a boy instead of a girl, then at the same age, she would have fitted the specification. Bachchu is twelve. If the revolution or the anarchy doesn't end in another three years or so, then he'll have to worry about Bachchu as well.

Aditya's jaws stiffen as he suppresses a yawn. His head feels heavy. He can't think any more.

Pritha is in the other room. She comes back to take the pair of shoes from Aditya and hands over his kurta-pyjama. "What're you waiting for? Take a wash and change your clothes."

"Yes, I'm going."

"Want to eat anything?"

"No. They gave dinner coupons at Bombay airport. I took a bite." Aditya's eyes are now on the darkness in Pritha–Bacchu's room. Though his gaze is on Bacchu, he is not really looking at him. His thoughts are more distant than hazy. He stands at the same place and asks, "Any news about your college opening?"

"No. I don't think it'll open in a hurry."

Aditya doesn't seem to hear her.

Her father's tall, strong build looks different from behind. This seems to be his genuine posture, turning his back to everything for the moment. A strange silence pervades all over the body—as if he will carry his very own world and go off somewhere or will get detached from everything around him. Just a while ago, this same man was hitting his knees with his fists at the news of the shooting, his eyes had become so intense in reaction! Unbelievable that this same man leaves for work on the dot at nine; talks non-stop in English in his air-conditioned chamber; flies on tour to Bombay, Delhi, Madras, Bangalore or Trivandrum once or twice every month. This same man writes; pages after pages, pouring himself coffee from the flask all night; his writings are carried in well-known publications, printed as books, he must have a lot of readers—otherwise why do even unknown people query when they hear his name, the writer? This is her father, known to her for ages. Yet, why does he seem so unfamiliar and distant at times? Why does it feel that the blood relation is simply incidental—in reality Baba is an island within himself!

At this moment, as she watches Aditya enter the toilet, kurta-pyjama in hand, Pritha thinks: True, there were problems, but Baba's home after four days—Ma should have returned tonight.

The heart is a dangerous thing, once it falls in the slush, it's difficult to drag it out. It's better to stay away from the slush, Aditya explains to himself so that he can rid himself of the worry. A relatively cushy job, financial security, and some recognition as a writer—these are not sufficient for being exceptional, cannot be. In spite of thousands of requests, the taxi driver refuses you—you have to run from one to the other with the same request, how are you different from the ordinary nameless man on Esplanade trying to somehow push himself into a bus, running hither and thither and ultimately failing? No, there's really no difference. Only power can make you different—power to give orders, to induce orders. If you don't have that power, you'll feel helpless facing all unfairness, blood will rush to your head, even a sleeping man will wake up at the sudden sound outside his own groove, where his power is futile. A little while ago, Aditya had realised this helplessness as he chatted with Pritha, his fists clenched in agitation. But the fact is, a strong man and a weak man both have fists—what is given as a little charity appears to be your right!

Many knots get untangled if you can laugh at yourself. Ease returns. The same happens now. Aditya splashes water on his face and head, changes his clothes and comes out of the toilet to see Pritha making his bed. Even though she told Sweta and Abdul what she had to, it's apparent that the girl was tense at not getting any certain information about her father's return. A person looks different when woken up from sleep abruptly—it's difficult to do anything diligently then, one is unwilling and lethargic, yawns, even the voice becomes drowsy. Ever since she opened the door, nothing of the sort has been noticeable in Pritha's face. Daytime normalcy and activity so late in the night. Now more active out of a sense of relief since the tension is over.

The sight of Pritha moving from one side of the bed to the other fills Aditya's heart with affection. He could have taken tomorrow's morning flight instead of tonight's. He had discarded the option in favour of his family. Now he feels he had taken the right decision; otherwise he would have missed the soothing company of his daughter, Sweta in this house. Other than some unwarranted worries, this night has gifted him some exceptional emotions. Office, tour, writing, parties—his days pass away in all there, how little time he has for them!

"Can I have some coffee, dear?"

"Coffee at this time of the night?" Pritha retorts from inside, "When'll you sleep then?"

"It's not night any more! Almost three-thirty." Aditya waits for Pritha to come out of the room. "At five I go for morning walk. Let me go early today—it'll be freshening."

Pritha looks straight at Aditya from a distance of three feet.

"Tired?"

"No. In fact, I'm feeling quite active. But, there's a strain of uncertainty, it strains your nerves."

"Sometimes you speak in the language of your characters." Pritha doesn't lose the chance of teasing her father, "You wait. I'll get your coffee."

Pritha goes to the kitchen to make coffee. Aditya returns to the living room.

I don't speak the language of my characters—I could have told Pritha, the characters speak my language. My experiences, emotions, sorrows give birth to whatever I could become but haven't, whatever I could get but didn't. And ultimately, they stand on their own feet. If the small fish huddled up together in the glass jar are poured in the larger space of the aquarium, they become restless, their fins are set free and they swim from one side to the other. They acquire their colours and fulfilment. And then they return to each other, come closer, love and attack each other. Each develops one's language; acquires one's means of survival—from the same water. Their blood groups become different. Even their behaviour. And then their social structure, their democracy gets disturbed. One scares the other because the other gets scared. One shoots a bullet so that the other is deprived of the opportunity to shoot.

No, I can't say all this.

Aditya finds himself incomprehensible. Not just today, at this moment; he often feels so. At times, he feels the impulse to drive himself by his own logic is greater than his honesty about it. Or there's no novelty in the language of his thoughts regarding his writing, or about the writer's reaction to the country, the society, politics or mankind. Many writers before him have thought the same way, many will think so. Society or mankind won't change a bit. Maybe it's also true that the language of thoughts is not the same as the language of reaction; and as long as the reaction doesn't become physical—direct some readers—they feel hungry by reading about hunger, they gulp down everything with their eyes, they haven't learnt the use of the mouth or teeth; words are their bread and butter. It's very easy to recongise them—they are his comrades. This murder of four young boys all of a sudden, thinking about them had stiffened his fists. That's about all. It didn't take long to unclench his fists. Because, by then he was taken up by the concern about his own security. What would have happened if Pritha wasn't a girl. Bacchu too would reach the same age of getting murdered, etc. With these worries, he'll go for his morning walk to the maidan a little later—the doctor had advised him to walk to keep fit when aeschemia was diagnosed a couple of years back. By the time he returns, the hawker'll have delivered the newspaper.

He'll read the Bengali and the English newspapers thoroughly, he feels immature if he misses out any bit of news that others know. And then he'll go to office in time. It's because of his job that he lives relatively luxuriously in Wood Street, the job allows him to write in his own way. Otherwise he would have had to write screenplays, adventure stories, travelogues and things like that for a living. He needs to write to keep himself alive. Besides, writing has brought him some sort of recognition and fame, the opportunity to be different from others. A longtime habit has developed into an anchorage. If human history is the history of development, then he too has developed from youth to maturity. The game is such that he now has to develop even further or else he has to draw a full stop, which is not possible. Of all the diseases, paralysis is the one that Aditya hates the most.

As he tries to stifle a long sigh, Aditya remembers a symbol. A flag on top of a temple. Its privileged positioning makes it distinctive. It somehow withstands sunshine, thunder, rain with ease; even though it may turn colourless, shredded or swayed, it's scared to leave the foundation of its existence. Gradually, it reaches its decay, if of course, a cyclone doesn't turn the holy structure of the temple into a ruin!

"Baba, why're you so disturbed?"

"Why?"

"You wanted coffee! And now you're not interested in it. That newspaper is yesterday's, stale. What are you so engrossed in?"

"Nothing. I was just glancing through."—Aditya avoids the topic as if he's caught redhanded. Pritha's comment makes him aware that his eyes are on the newspaper but he's actually reading himself. He sips the coffee with much vigour and says, "Good, very refreshing—"

"That's your imagination. A tired man can't get refreshed with just one sip."

Pritha's face is glum. To please her, Aditya takes another large sip and says, "You twitted me a little while ago. Now you're talking the language of my characters."

"You don't need to please me", Pritha says, "the coffee has obviously turned cold. No steam—I can see—"

Aditya smiles. Thank God she's his own daughter, or else it would be a definite case of neglect to ask for coffee and then let it go cold by irresponsible distraction. There's reason to be hurt.

"Why're you getting puffed up? Black cold coffee has a different taste, gives a different mood—"

"Your tastes can't have changed in four days." Pritha looks down as she speaks. And then suddenly says, "I know what you're thinking"

"What?"

"About Ma. Returning home after all the trouble and not finding Ma—"

"Come on, come on—" Aditya doesn't let Pritha proceed any further. In an amused tone, he says, "A clever girl shouldn't draw conclusions like that. You yourself said your grandfather's ill, you told her not to come back so late."

Pritha keeps quiet. He gulps down the coffee and says, "You're a simple girl, you try to build up an ideal situation. Baba'll return home, Ma'll open the door and then we'll all sit together and chat—"

Aditya stops at this point because he has to; he looks at his daughter closely.

"Am I not right, dear?"

Pritha keeps fiddling with her nightie in silence.

Aditya says, "Earlier when I was younger, I too thought like you. I was filled with expectations. Then I found there's no ideal situation, these are only perceptions of the ideal. It's impossible to put them together in a unified whole. Otherwise, my flight wouldn't be delayed, your grandfather wouldn't fall ill, it wouldn't rain so heavily, Abdul could have taken the car to pick up your mother if he had the correct information about the flight. None of these happened. How would your mother return?"

"I didn't think of all that when I asked."

" I know. It wouldn't be your fault even if you did. I was distracted by something else—I can't explain it to you. Maybe you'll understand when you grow up, you'll know that a man is not born to be happy in the security within the four walls. He has to move out to a bigger arena—which is called society. Even there, nothing is ideal. This tug-of-war between the home and the world is disturbing. You feel lost—helpless!

A faint sound approaches from a distance. It grows in volume just as Aditya completes his monologue. Another car is speeding past, right across their house. The street dogs are awakened by the noise—some crows flutter and flow away in the sky cawing in chorus.

Pritha had moved to the balcony at the noise. After the car leaves, she leans across the railing, looks this way and that and turns back to Aditya.

"Police van."

"I guessed so—"

Aditya stands up. He stretches out his arms and approaches his daughter. He touches Pritha's shoulders gently and says, "It must be past four o'clock. You've been awake too long, go to bed. You'll feel sick otherwise—"

Pritha leans out again. That same posture—as if to see as far as her sight goes. And then says, "Why are police vans passing by so frequently?"

Aditya broods and looking at the street, says, "Maybe they run around like this every night. We've noticed today because we're awake. We wouldn't have known if we were asleep."

The sky is darkening one last time before the break of dawn. Aditya can't see a single star in the sky; no moonlight either. It strikes him that it's waning time of the moon. Lightening flashes across the sky, so there's cloud too. Not a whiff of breeze. After the prolonged rain since evening, it is now dry. August is the peak of the rainy season. It may start raining again any time.

Pritha yawns. The odour of her breath flows out of her mouth.

"You are very sleepy. Now go to bed."

"I'm going" Pritha prepares to leave on her own. "You could have slept a little too."

"I said, there's no need. Let the sky clear up, I'll go out."

"Shut the main door properly. The key's on the bookshelf."

Pritha has almost gone. Aditya calls after her.

"Were there any phone calls for me?"

"Sekhar Dutta from your office." She tries to remember and says, "And yes, I forgot. Debu Chaudhury from 'Our Times' had called last evening. He wants you to get in touch with him as soon as you get back."

"Alright."

When Pritha leaves, there is no trace of her presence anywhere around. He feels light-headed. This feeling of emptiness doesn't take shape usually. Office, writing, family are so enmeshed together that none of these are identifiable individually. In fact, all the unnerving worries that have been bothering him are also not there any more. Sweta comes to his mind once—her face, body and sweet odour but the thought flitters away before it actually touches his feelings.

Aditya stands in the balcony for some time looking at the sky. Even though the colour of the sky remains unchanged, the symptoms of dawn unravel gradually. Birds start chattering at a distance, a light is turned on in a ground floor room of the ship-like house across the park. Two men are cycling down the street lazily—their faint voices can be heard because of the eerie silence. Far away, where the sky seems to touch the earth, a faint red streak emerges from the darkness of the sky. Just as a taxi honks across from the south to the north, another sound becomes audible—on the ground floor itself. Someone is starting a car. In a couple of minutes, the watchman busies himself to open the gate—a white ambassador leaves. Although he can't recognise the passenger, it's not difficult to guess that it's someone to catch the morning flight, on way to the airport. Aditya knows that in their thirty-two flats in the multi-storeyed building, someone or other leaves as early as this every day. He doesn't know all names, doesn't even recognise all by face. A couple of years ago, when a plane had crashed near Delhi and the list of casualties was given in the papers, he came to know that one of them was his neighbour. About ten days later, the flat bell rang and he opened the door to find a desolate young girl standing. The girl held the funeral card in her hand. She introduced herself and said, "Baba was very fond of your writing. He wanted to get introduced to you. That's why Ma said—if you can make it to his funeral rites—" The girl broke down as she said this. As he consoled the young fatherless girl, Aditya felt she was crying out of suppressed anger. Aditya, whom her father knew so well, didn't even know about his existence in spite of living so close by—she felt insulted.

Before darkness clears up, morning walkers are out on the road. And then the thoughts come. Death is such a strange thing—as he walks briskly down the lonely Moira Street, Lord Sinha Road and Chowringhee Road, he thinks no one knows where death is waiting for whom. Sometimes a death makes you feel that you should have known the person. Maybe your outlook would change, maybe your life too. You might get some new shelter.

The wayward thoughts engross him. He can't concentrate on the walk. Yet, as he approaches the green of the Maidan, his nerves get rejuvenated at the touch of the morning breeze. He takes in the fresh air and looks around in unmindful thoughts, but he has to stop all of a sudden. At a little distance away, towards the western end of the Maidan, the headlights of a vehicle slowly fade into the darkness. As the shape becomes a little visible, he realises it's a police van. A thin tall man gets down and starts running—some more men follow. And then bullet shots. The man falls down.

A few moments pass. And then Aditya starts running wildly.

Chapter 2

Slender fingers running through his hair, shaking his jaws lightly and then a gentle kiss on his forehead—Aditya wakes up at these familiar touches. He sees Sweta lying with her head on the pillow next to him, where she was supposed to have been last night. The reason for her not being there at night is not unknown to him. Now prim and proper, bathed, in fresh clothes, the meticulously drawn red bindi on the forehead—together it's enough to immerse him in her charm. Sweta has more or less managed to maintain her figure in spite of the regular exploits on her body for twenty one years. Aditya should have got used to her beauty by now but Sweta is adept at peeping to keep her mystery alive.

Aditya sits up. He can see the Japanese wall clock straight ahead. Of course, he should have guessed the time from the brightness in the room.

The thought drives him to another conjecture.

It was a few minutes past five when he had slumped on the bed to stifle his fear and anxiety—Pritha was fast asleep, Bachchu was lying in the same posture as before, the flat was dark though the sun was rising. Unless there's something urgent, Satya doesn't come up from the servants' quarters before six. So, nobody noticed his return. In the meantime, he has been sleeping for almost three hours. Fatigue and worries sometimes act like morphia.

Sweta's face is turned the other way. Aditya can see her from waist downwards. Fair, too fair—few Bengali women are as fair as she. Only embarrassment can cause roses to bloom on her cheeks, Aditya sometimes has a light-hearted notion that the name Mahasweta fits her since the word Sweta means fair. The metaphor touches him again. The bare feet out of the paisley-bordered striped saree pulls his sight upwards. Any other day, in normal times—especially after five days of being away, desire would have taken hold of Aditya. But at this moment, the attraction of her body don't take shape; his body doesn't react. Trying to arouse himself, he remains unaffected.

Sweta observes Aditya for a few seconds.

"Won't you go to office?"

"I'll go." Aditya turns towards his wife. As he steps down from the bed, he asks, "When did you get back?"

"At seven. Got an empty bus. Knee-deep water that side—" Sweta sits up. Seeing Aditya unmindful, she says in a guilty tone, "It was raining so heavily, I thought you wouldn't be back."

Aditya stops in front of the mirror. Sweta can see half of his face. A man's look doesn't change in four-five days. But, to Sweta, Aditya appears slightly different. It's not possible to make out how though. He's quiet by nature;

speaks little and that too, weighing each word—one has to guess at what he's thinking from the expression in his eyes. One might take him to be a snob at first sight, Aditya might appear to be keeping aloof from others. But Sweta knows from her twenty-one years of experience that it's not true. His appearance is not his real self. "It's very easy to misunderstand Aditya"—Kanchan had once said, "You know Sweta, you can get to know your husband through the camera, such an innocent face is rare". Sweta smiled, "I didn't look through the camera when I married him."

But it's true that Aditya's reticence worries her at times. She feels, like a lot of others things, that Aditya has simply taken their relationship for granted; that's why though there's interest in the give and take, there's no intensity. Like it's now. She can make out that there are no likes or dislikes associated with Aditya's distraction—he's thinking of something which he would have been, had Sweta not been here.

Sweta gathers courage and says, "Baba fell ill all of a sudden yesterday—"

"Pritha told me—" Aditya moves away from the mirror to the window. "He's okay now?"

"More or less. He had to be put on oxygen for about three hours."

The layout of the house is such that only the east is visible from this window.

Numerous tall buildings have cropped up to restrict vision. The road or the pavement, the tin-roofed congested slum are all hidden away. When they moved here from

Bhowanipore about ten years ago, it wasn't only the sky that was visible. You could see the huge cemetery across Rawdon Street, the Lower Circular Road cutting through Park Street and so much more. Now one can only assume these to be there. New flats are bringing in new neighbours, living in such tall buildings makes one used to the clear blue sky, the bright horizons. Some time ago, flipping through the pages of a financial journal, he had come across a survey—in nine major Indian cities, less than five per cent of the population lives in these posh houses or flats, most of the expensive consumer goods are produced for these people. For the rest, there's no difference between the economic condition of rural or urban life—they have a hand-to-mouth existence. This is the history of our development from colonialism to independence. The stray thoughts touch Aditya, with no definite feeling of anger or shame. He knows from his own life that the wall of survival of this five per cent is the most fragile, it might crack at the slightest blow so there's a continuous effort to paint it, climb upwards all the time.

His thoughts take him away from his immediate surroundings. Time stands still.

He comes back to reality at Sweta's voice.

"What're you waiting for? Shall I get you tea?"

"Yeah!"

Aditya hurries. He goes to the toilet and starts brushing his teeth. He ruminates, Pritha's room is to the west. If you stand at the window, you can only guess at the direction of the Maidan. Nothing more.

He comes out of the toilet and to the living room. Sweta

brings the tea herself. She calls Pritha. It's difficult to wake her up. Bacchu must be engrossed in the sports page of the newspaper. Seeing his father, he gives him the two newspapers. A simple, childish face—he'll now be at his books for some time and then get ready for school. Sweta is instructing Satya in the kitchen. The normal family life is gradually returning. As he glances at the front page of the newspaper, Aditya thinks, it's actually Sweta who runs the family. Really that the course of events would have been different if Sweta was home last night—he would have gone to bed soon after returning home, take some time to fall asleep and wake up late. Which means there would be no chance of going for a morning walk before sunrise. And then everything would happen as in routine. To make the night's sleep peaceful, newspapers arrive in the morning— another piece of news would have been added to all the other news or maybe it wouldn't. Who knows!

It's not difficult to roll back three hours or more if you are comatose. Aditya relives the entire scene.

Even in the darkness, Aditya had seen clearly that the man was thin and tall. He had got off the van first—alone, some others followed soon, he couldn't make out how many. The man had started running and the distance between him and the others had increased. Aditya felt that there was nothing but sheer desperation in his disorderly run. Just then the bullets were fired and he fell down instantaneously.

He didn't know what happened consequently. Before he realised that this was a planned murder, he had trembled and got on his feet—along Chowringhee, to no particular direction faster than his but normal speed, almost blindly.

When he reached Theatre Road and saw at a distance few men and cars, he felt safe. He turned back for the first time but the Maidan was beyond vision. An empty taxi approached from the opposite direction. He stopped it and hopped inside. Straight to Wood Street, home. He handed over a five-rupee note to the taxi driver, didn't wait for the change—walked to the lift, ignoring the surprised stare of the watchman. The liftman doesn't come before six, so he had to press the button himself. He reached the flat and almost pressed the calling bell when he realised he was going to make the first mistake. He had taken the keys on Pritha's advice—no need to wake up everybody by pressing the bell. Besides, what was there to be so nervous about? He hadn't murdered anybody; there was no curfew so there was no question of breaking rules. It's a civic right to go for morning walks according to one's wish and in the process he had witnessed a murder. Had there been or gap of two to five minutes, he wouldn't have seen it but the incident would have happened in any case. It's nothing new in Calcutta or West Bengal or India. There's no positive statistics with regard how many men have been killed between 1965 to this 1971—just day before yesterday four youth had been killed in Beleghata canalside. The witnesses to the incident had informed the police, the Writers Buildings and the Press. Then why is he, Aditya Ray, a name which many recongise as a writer, getting so worked up? Why did he run back then? Shouldn't he have yelled out, gathered people around and run to the spot—where possibly the bullet-hit man was still struggling for life? Or, is it that all his conscience can do is to get him agitated at newspaper reports and then if necessary, to get together with some people and sign protest letters?

Gradually, he breathes normally. Doesn't take long to come to a decision.

Deputy Commissioner Ashok Dutta is a friend. They were together at the University. Met him last in July, at a party at Grand Hotel thrown by a Consulate. They had spoken about the strained times though Ashok didn't want to divulge much. He had said, "My own cousin has been missing for a month. He was arrested in Seuri with some others. My uncle came to me desparately for some news. I'm helpless. What can I do really? Conscience and job are not the same. And remember, it's not the police alone who are killing. Those who want to change the system, tell them to strike at the right place. They haven't yet mudered a single industrialist or minister." Seeing Ashok so agitated, Aditya had said, "Will that solve the problem?" "May not but—" Ashok continued in the same tone, "the politics will change its course, they should hate those who ought to be hated. Don't hate me just because I'm in the police service. My son Sudip—he's in Presidency—doesn't talk to me these days. Because, two of his friends were killed by the police and I am in the service." The conversation didn't proceed any further. Seeing Sweta approaching, Ashok forced a smile, "Boudi how are you?"

This morning, coming to a decision, Aditya remembers Ashok. He can inform Ashok about the incident.

Trembling with excitement, Aditya picks up the receiver but stops before dialling. What's the point, he hesitates, in informing Ashok about this murder over 'phone—Ashok'll hear him and then forget all about it. Maybe he'll advise him not to get agitated about all this. Aditya doesn't want that. He wants to get the details of what he saw to be recorded so that the incident which occurred in the dark comes out in the open, becomes a subject of conversation, reaction and protest. He can inform the Press; he has many journalists friends. But, Aditya reminds himself immediately, if the incident is circulated through the media, he might be asked why he approached them instead of reporting to the police. They may also say that the entire story is imaginary and fictitious—nothing of that sort had happened and there's nothing but self-publicity in this.

The thoughts and the logic come to him sequentially. By the time he takes a decision, he looks through the directory, finds the number of the Park Street Police Station and calls.

The O.C. himself responds. Aditya introduces himself distinctly and describes the incident. The man retorts in a taunting tone, "That's absurd. I made a round in that area half an hour back. Are you sure you didn't dream about it?"

"I'm not joking. It's a fact", Aditya says as rudely as possible, "I've seen it with my own eyes. I can't say who the man was but it was a case of brutal murder."

"This is not Beleghata or Baranagar, it's Chowringhee. I don't know what you're talking about."

"You don't have to know. You just record the case. I'll inform the Press too."

"That you can. You seem to have high connections. What's the address you said?"

Aditya gives his address.

"Mr Ray, another question—" The O.C. says abruptly, "the time you mentioned was pitch dark. That's not really the time for a morning walk."

"That's an irrelevant question."

Aditya disconnects the 'phone. And tells himself, this was necessary. After this, it doesn't matter if the police denies his informing them. One is accountable only to one's own conscience.

Earlier, while flipping through the newspaper Aditya would only read for himself. Now, he actually looks for news. Today's paper doesn't have any more news about murders. Much of the front page is taken up by Bangladesh and description of the excellent law and order situation in West Bengal under President's Rule since June. In the inside pages, the statements of the opposition party about the shooting inside Dum Dum jail. They've argued clearly that there's only one motive for entrusting the Detective Department of Calcutta Police with the duty of dealing with the Naxalites and that is to give it immense power to kill. The Naxalites won't be treated as members of any political party any more. To the government, they are simply murderers or criminals and they'll be dealt with as such.

"Baba, you are incorrigible."

Pritha. She doesn't look as if she is just out of bed. A few drops of water near her ears, cheeks and chin give away that she has just washed. She walks in with her cup of tea.

Aditya smiles at his daughter.

"Why?"

"You didn't sleep all night. And now you're already sitting with the papers."

Sweta must have been nearby. Before Aditya can reply, she quips, "Didn't he sleep! I woke him up."

"Really!" Pritha exclaims. "But you told me you wouln't sleep. You wanted to go for a morning walk."

Aditya is trapped. But he can't tell them about the morning incident. They'll worry unnecessarily, might even advise him to stop going for morning walks. Sweta can't keep anything to herself, she visits a few neighbours in this building—it's not impossible that others might come to know. He decides to evade.

"Both you and your mother are right. I wanted to go out but I felt so sleepy, I thought—"

"The telephone's ringing." Pritha gets up. She returns to inform, "It's your phone. Kanchan Uncle wants to speak to you."

As he gets up, he is weak in his knees, his waist is aching, the entire body feels heavy. Why! Maybe because of the long haul early in the morning. He can't remember running like that since his college days.

The telephone is in the study. Before picking up the receiver, Aditya pulls aside the curtains to let light come in.

"Hello—"

"Good Morning, Kanchan."

"Yeah. How are you?"

Kanchan pauses a while to say, "Why's your voice so heavy? Have I woken you up?"

"No, I got up some time back."

"How was the trip?"

Aditya can't help smiling. Every time he returns from a trip, Kanchan asks him the same question with the same eagerness. Maybe he imagines he is being smart. He says, "Usual. Nothing exciting. But I returned late—the flight was delayed."

"I know. Last night's rain was disastrous. I took a lot of snaps of waterlogging."

"So, what's new?"

"Nothing much, carrying on." Kanchan says, "I saw your interview in the literary number of *Sankha*."

"Really! It's out?"

"No, it'll hit the stands in a day or two. I went to their office yesterday. Saw the advance copy."

"Oh—"

"I must say—" Kanchan hesitates, "you are one of the four-five writers they've given major coverage to. But it's not very favourable to you. There are a few remarks which I didn't like."

"Why?"

"It might give the impression that your job is more important to you—it doesn't give you time to write, that's why you're not more prolific, you write only occasionally—that sort of thing.

"Writers are not chickens that they'll be judged by the number of eggs they hatch."

Aditya is exasperated. He takes the receiver in the other

hand and says, "Besides, I didn't tell them all that."

"Yes, yes, I know. It's their way of explaining your not being prolific."

"I know how it's happened, Kanchan, Dhruva Nandi took my novel 'The War' to publish serially but ultimately didn't carry it. Apparently a lot of people would be antagonised, his job would be at stake. He wanted a plain romantic novel that readers would gulp down. From then on that time I don't write for them. When they asked for the interview, I thought they were trying to normalise the relationship—so I agreed."

His jaws stiffen as he speaks. Once more changing hands to hold the receiver, he turns around and says, "They'll lose face in the intellectual world if they can't give this explanation for my not writing for them. You know my background, Kanchan, you know how I suffered. They'll never accept that day after day they didn't publish me and in the process blacked me out—because I refused to be 'yes man'."

"I'm sorry, Adityada." Kanchan says, embarrassed, "I shouldn't have told you about it."

"No, no. You did the right thing. Did Dhruva Nandi say anything else?"

"No, just that he hasn't seen you for a long time, why you don't write more and things like that. But your photograph came out very well. You know, that's by me?"

"Yes, you had told me." The nine o'clock siren blew. Aditya should have been ready by now.

"That rolling mills assignment is through. I've seen the

contact print, it's come out alright. Can you spare some time today?"

"Come over. Any time after lunch. I'll be in."

He feels low as he puts down the receiver. He has to find out how much of what Kanchan said is true. But Kanchan must have seen the issue. Dhruva Nandi's association is suspicious. He has known Dhruva for a long time and he can guess that Dhruva does not indulge in anything without a purpose. Is it possible that the interview was a ruse, to stew him in his own juice? Not impossible. One has to see the context in which the implications are drawn. But, if what Kanchan said is true, it might appear that writing is just a hobby for him—not his own breath, his last resort for survival; if there is a choice between his job and writing he'll probably choose the job! Yet, his years as a writer are longer than that of his marriage or his children. And certainly longer than his job.

He remembers he didn't accept a job in a suburban college after his M.A. simply for his writing—he preferred to be in Calcutta and took up a modest job as a part-time school teacher. He was born in this city, grew up with its sights and sounds, he had been writing about its people, their lives and their mentalities—if he left this city, he would have to leave them behind; his roots and his heritage would be lost. He realised from later experience that his decision had more emotion than practical truth. A writer is born in his own blood; through various feelings and experiences the same blood is churned up again and again. Then, why should a writer die with a change of location? Rather, inner vision adds to the outer experience; many more doors and windows open up. This way, for almost thirty odd years, he has been thrilled by the birth of words after words from his pen. In them he has seen the birth and death of mankind. And now you wish to describe that as a mere hobby? This is fraud, betrayal, conspiracy!

As he walks out of the study, Aditya observes something strange. A little earlier, the atmosphere was totally different—there is utter silence now in the entire flat. Sweta is chopping vegetables with great concentration. Pritha's eyes are on the newspaper but she doesn't seem to be reading. Bachchu is sprawled across the bed reading Tintin. Even the sound of pots and pans in the kitchen—which Aditya had heard when he entered the study—has stopped and Satya is busy cleaning rice.

Aditya is lost. Without addressing anyone in particular, he calls out, "What's wrong? Why're you all so silent?" Aditya sounds apologetic, contrary to his nature.

"By your words!" Sweta turns to Aditya and says, "What's there to be so upset about in what somebody has written somewhere?"

"Did I shout too much? It reached you too?" Aditya is embarrassed. He looks at Pritha. "What do you have to say?"

"You're very tense, Baba. I noticed it at night. You never get so agitated."

"Who knows!" Aditya moves ahead and plonks down on the sofa. Forcing a smile, he says, "I suddenly felt so insulted."

"You're really a character." Pritha says, "*Sankha* is not the only magazine around. People are not so stupid as to believe all that's written."

Pritha stops to think. Watching Aditya, she says, "Have you seen the latest issue of the *Illustrated Weekly*? There's a four-page article on modern Bengali novels, by Subodh Mitra. He has written quite a bit on you. If you were a nobody he would have left you out."

"Maybe. If you say, then it's definitely so." Aditya tries to relax. "Where's the magazine?"

"I'll get it."

Pritha runs to the study. Sweta yells out to her, "And show your father the snaps too. He hasn't seen them."

"Bacchu, bring the snaps for Baba." Pritha comes back with a rolled up *Illustrated Weekly*. "Look at page number 26."

Bacchu brings an envelope full of snaps. Sweta comes forward. Aditya glances through the magazine and keeps it away. He picks up the envelope. A bunch of coloured photographs—Sweta in different moods, Pritha, Bachchu—in different locales in Calcutta. Kanchan's photography, obviously.

Even with his eyes on the snaps, Aditya realises he's not looking at them. The dark Maidan is returning to him. A thin tall man, many chasing him. Bullets. Aditya looks around at his family desparately and tries to hide himself. He says to himself: All of you keep me in your midst, please.

Chapter 3

Four days later, at office, Aditya feels out of joint at the sound of rains. Looking at the rainwater splashing on the frosted glass panes of the window, he assures himself that since there has been no news in the papers for three days, there probably won't ever be. The Beleghata incident was reported within twenty-four hours. From morning to morning, ninety-six hours have passed since the Maidan incident. News gets stale, it catches fungus. The same will probably happen to this. The dark will remain dark.

It depresses him. Exasperated also. A lump comes up his throat and trails down his chest. The rainwater on the window panes gathers and vaporises—the walls seem to come closer. Yet, he can visualise the scene clearly—at Maidan just where his eyes are fixed now, there, on the green tall grass, washed by the rainwater continuously.

That day, if the man had not fallen down when shot at or if he had the chance to run a little further, he would have reached him. For a moment, their eyes would have met and before falling down, the man could have thought that at least one person had remained witness to his murder. Or it could also be that his silence in the lonely helplessness would have found its voice at the sight of him and he would have cried "help". Though he has never faced situations like these, people say that face to face with death, man clings on to that solitary word. It might also be that along with the man, the killers would have spotted him as well and since the murder was supposed to have been executed in the dark solitude, keeping no witness—sooner or later he would also have been killed the same way. Then the entire course of events would change and he has no clue to what could or would have happened. Is it ominous that none of these happened except what he saw? Does he have any other responsibility as a human being?

Not only today, the question has been haunting him for the last four days. He has always been brooding this far and halting abruptly to return to it later. The same happens now. Aditya realises in embarrassment that the answer eludes him.

There's no reason to believe that any action has followed his impulsive phone call to the Park Street police station. He has also kept the entire thing to himself. He hasn't spoken to his family or to the Press. He has even hesitated to tell Ashok though the thought recurred to him a few times. But since that day, he has been feeling time and again that he's not the same person any more.

The only silver lining is that he's by nature a self-engrossed person so he doesn't appear too abnormal outwardly. In the mean time, his daily routine is unchanged so nobody would realise that Aditya is going through a crisis. He wakes up before dawn, washes and goes for his morning walk. He takes almost the same route every day. There's a faint light even before sunrise, some people walk past him. Buses and trams start plying much earlier, taxis and cars speed towards the Howrah station, hospitals or elsewhere. The touch of fresh air is felt only at this time. As he walks a little further, Aditya's speed slackens and his eyesight grows keen and though nobody notices, his vision gets transfixed at a particular spot. And then, returning home, as he flips through the newspaper over a cup of tea, none can realise that though his eyes are on Bangladesh, President's Rule, a boy's drowning in a pond, imprisonment for a minor girl's rape, he's actually looking for one particular bit of news. Even when he speaks to Sweta, Pritha or Bachchu on trivialities, he remains detached in an unusual way—he feels whoever he's talking to are distant even though they might be closely related to him. For some strange reason, the one who's actually close to him is that man—he is thin and tall, that's all he knows about the man, his face was covered in darkness. Yet, in spite of the haziness, the few moments have created a deep bond between them, which Aditya cannot erase even if he tries to.

A while ago, the advertising people left after the presentation of the corporate campaign. The copy file along with the brief is lying on the desk. Not being able to concentrate on it, Aditya closes the file and watches the window panes turn hazy with the rainwater. Without much of a thought, he rises and approaches the window. He wipes a portion of the glass with his bare hands. When he presses his forehead over that, the cool smooth feeling relaxes him. The horizon looks opaque in the heavy rain. The Telephone

Bhavan, the Writers Buildings on the right are all wet. It's not possible to make out whether there are people on the streets. Two double-decker buses turn towards the GPO. These too get obscured by the torrential shower. As he tries to breathe normally, he feels time is a great healer—it can cover up a lot things. A man—whoever he is—survives in the Corporation death register and in the memories of his near and dear ones, the range of memories determine his place in posterity. Beyond these, all memories are momentary and incident-specific. If the incidents are significant, the memories gain importance. In this case, it's not possible to know the identity of the murdered man—not even that of his immediate kin. And since the entire incident occurred almost out of sight of anyone and in the thick of darkness—there's no news of any dead body in the Maidan either—it's of no significance. The problem is with the word 'almost'. Since the incident didn't occur totally out of sight, the responsibility of making it public and giving it the importance due to it, is his. His and his alone. Instead, only by informing the police, aren't you trying to shirk responsibility? Why? Fear of death? Or, fearing that other nitty-gritties might be associated with this? The Beleghata incident had come out in the open because there were many witnesses and in this case, it's you alone. Then, it can it be assumed that *you*, the writer who belongs to and yet is different from the common man, that same *you* can't take the risk of exposing a crime for some reason or the other? How are you different!

Aditya gathers his stray thoughts at the ring of the telephone. He returns to his chair, lets the phone ring one more time and picks up the receiver.

"Hello."

"Mr Ray, have I disturbed you?"

Paresh Som, Account Director of Creative Consultant, on the line. Aditya assumes that he wants to know about the presentation. He asks normally, "When did you get back? It's raining cats and dogs this side."

"It's raining here too but not so hard." Paresh asks, "How's the reaction?"

"Not bad. Should be okay."

"Shoud be! You seem to have reservations."

"No. The creative work is quite good."

"Thank you. Do you know the MD's opinion? What does he say?"

Aditya replies, "Not yet. I might get to know tomorrow."

"Alright sir." Paresh says after a while, "We were discussing your comments on the research findings—on our way back. Frankly, I still don't understand the reason for your objections."

"My objection is not to the findings but the interpretation."

Aditya shifts in his chair. The same reaction which had excited him during the presentation in the conferences room an hour ago returns. The reaction loses its sharpness if repeated over and over. He ponders on what to say and then continues, "I don't see any reason to withdraw what I said earlier. The problem, Mr Som, is that people who deal with marketing and advertising in our country don't keep in touch with the socio-political perspective—they frame their classification, judge people's mental framework without analysing the economic or social conditions."

"I don't understand."

"How else can I explain!" Aditya grows irritated. He controls himself, "You tried to interpret, those who are turning towards terelyne trousers are all broad-minded and those who still wear cotton are conservative. It didn't strike you that the phenomenon is related more to economic capability than to mentality."

"I understand." Paresh's voice sounds sarcastic. He says, "But Sir, the job of advertisement is to sell goods, sell image—to judge people's mentality, rather than their economic capability, and determine strategy accordingly. Even people who can't afford wear terelyne. That's the success of advertisement."

"Maybe. If you say, then it must be so." Aditya mutters between his teeth. "I need to learn advertisement from you."

"You're getting upset."

"No. Carry on."

"I admit there's some truth in what you say. But you must realise if we don't restrict our area then we'll have to rely on conjectures."

Paresh is trying to be evasive, Aditya realises. He says, "Restricting the area and wrong interpretation are not the same, Mr Som. There's a sort of snobbery in branding those who can't afford to follow fashion. I came to know from your research that there's something called Silly Rock, thirty per cent of College and University students are fans of these. Who are these students? Are they in Calcutta? In West Bengal? Then what about those who have risked their lives and career to change the system—and are getting killed by the police?"

"I understand what you mean. But Sir, they don't read advertisements."

Aditya stops. His words are becoming weak. He has realised there's no point in discussing all this. Before ending the call, he says,"Thanks for calling. Give me a couple of days. I'll let you know our decision."

There is an addiction to the monotonous sound of rain. Once your ears and brain get used to it, you tend to forget how it was earlier. It's the same now. But he can make out it's not raining any more because he can hear vehicles passing. Aditya notices the window pane which he had wiped earlier has turned hazy again. After the rain, lines of water are gliding down the frame of the pane. Looking at the window intently, Aditya tries to remember his schedule for today. The Managing Director will address the Annual General Meeting of the Association of the Young Enterpreneurs—he had given him the points. Aditya has to prepare the entire lecture by this week. He had given the draft to be typed to the secretary. He has to enquire about the progress. And there's lots more. He glances at the diary and thinks, there's no end to the continuity. Wonder how he was so distracted.

It was about twelve when they had come out of the Conference Room. It's almost half past twelve now. Except for the five-to-seven-minute conversation with Paresh, the entire stretch of time had been lost in brooding. As the thought comes back, he presses the intercom button.

His secretary Chitra at the other end.

Aditya says, "Come in, I have to give you some dictation."

"Okay." Chitra says, "Mr Ray, there's a visitor for you. He has been waiting for quite time."

"Visitor!" He notices the visitor's slip under the paperweight. "Oh yes, I forgot. Send him in."

A consumptive man, in dhoti-kurta, wearing thick glasses. A few streaks of grey in the hair. The age is indecipherable from his appearance but his stubble proves that he doesn't shave more than twice or thrice a week. Men like these can be spotted around the book bazaar in College Street. Adiya remembers he hasn't been that side for quite some time. His new novel is in the press. The publisher Shyamapadababu had requested him to flip it through before he left for Bombay. He hadn't been able to. The last he had been to there was about a month back. The fact was, he had tried to go. As he reached Eden Hospital, the chaos and bomb blasts forced Abdul to turn the car back. He returned home to find Pritha not back yet. He was so nervous—Aditya didn't wait for even a minute. He rushed downstairs. The anger and frustration turned into tension, his affection taking priority over everything else. He walked up to the tram line, Pritha's route back. Trams had stopped. He walked back to the gate. Just then Pritha walked up from the south, somewhat lost, grim face. She raised her red eyes and said, "Tear gas—I couldn't see a thing. Went to Sealdah and took a train to Ballygunge." And then continued, "Soumen of our class was shot in the belly—" He took a long look at his daughter and said, "Tear gas or did you cry?" Pritha said, "You can't cry at times like these, Baba. I was trembling in anger." He read about the rest in the newspaper the next day—the clash between students and the police in front of Presidency College. One was killed. But his name wasn't Soumen.

"Recognise me?" The man pulls up a chair before Aditya asks him to. He says, "I'm Benoybhusan Hazra. I visited you at your house once."

The way he pronounces his name, introduces himself— the man seems faintly familiar. Aditya looks at him with creased brow, but can't remember whether it was at home that he had met a man like this. He asks, "Yes, what was it about?"

"Baikuntha Library. Silver Anniversary. Does it ring a bell?"

"Alright. What do I have to do?"

"Today's eighth. The function is on twenty-seventh. Thursday. You're the Chief Guest. You told me to remind you before the function, that's why I'm here. I have to get the cards printed."

Aditya asks, "Did I agree to come?"

"If you did, I would've got the cards printed." Benoy Hazra explains, "I've come to get your consent."

"Weekdays are a problem. Besides, I might have to go on tour at that time—"

Aditya looks at the sun ray filtering through the window, "You can't leave me out?"

"Why can't I? I've been running the library alone for twenty-five years—I can organise the function on my own too. A lot of members are your fans, they wanted you. That's why I had to come. I read literature a bit—I have no interest in seeing how writers look like."

"That's highly interesting." Aditya is genuinely curious, "You are very forthright."

Benoy Hazra stares through the thick lens. He doesn't reply.

"Where did you say your library was?

"Beleghata."

Aditya says, "A few days back four young men were—"

Before he's able to conclude, Benoy Hazra says, "Not four. There were five. The newspapers don't report correctly. They write what they are told. One dead body was already thrown in the van."

Aditya is silent.

Benoy Hazra looks around the chamber. Just the time it needed to see the whole room. And then comments abruptly, "Aren't you a communist?"

"What do you mean?"

"It seems so from your writing."

Chitra pushes the door and comes in. Seeing Aditya busy with the man, she goes out, saying, "Please call me when you're free."

"Okay."

It can usually be guessed from a visitor's appearance how long he might take. That's why Chitra had taken a chance. She turns back. This man is taking more time than he should have. His gait gives the feeling that he's a little cracked in the head. He should better leave now. Aditya throws hints.

"Is my writing branded?"

"Not really. But why shouldn't it be?" Benoy Hazra says, "Those who call you bourgeoise say so because of your job, the air-conditioned room, your manner of speech. Not because of your writing."

"I understand." Aditya leans back in his chair and says, "Call me up tomorrow or day after. I'll tell you whether I can make it or not."

"I'll do that." Benoy Hazra stands up. "Tomorrow I'll go to my daughter at Halishahar. I'll call you day after. Around this time, right?"

Aditya nods and sees the man leaving the room without waiting.

Strange man! Or, is it that all men are strange? Till a while ago, he had no idea about the existence of this man. He mentioned he had been to his house once. Even if he had been, he must not have spoken so much then. Aditya wouldn't have indulged him today then. But, on a second thought, Aditya thinks, the man may not be entirely crazy. Did he try to communicate something through his babble in the short span of time—some find him a communist and others think he's a bourgeois, did he try to tell him that? The words have no weight, they tremble in the slightest of breeze. But they occupy space. He might have picked up the words from others, or it might be a figment of his imagination. Are they new to Aditya! Some mistaken analyses here and there have built up the thought process of the writer, with which the writer's soul has no real attachment. The tensions arising from various incidents have diverted the stream of human relations, different reactions are born. The present reaction is driving towards the future possibilities. What is today a mere incident—blurred, maybe charming—will turn into history tomorrow. His job is to handle the reaction of men in the blurred or charming surroundings. As far as he knows himself, that's all the idea that he has when he writes. Whatever reaction one has, his own belief moulds it into words after words. If someone bursts into protest or revolt—tries to change the shape of the future, then will the changed future become part of the mainstream? He, Aditya Ray, hasn't changed—some change has occurred in his mindset and outlook, and definitely experiences, but not by transfusing new blood in place of old. Not by trimming the continuity of memories. The new Aditya Ray can still recoginse the old Aditya Ray.

Then?

Aditya loses his train of thought. He has remained firm in his belief even when he has analysed himself for so long—he hasn't failed to analyse, hasn't felt helpless. The day he does so, he'll have to look for a support system. Then, he might need one of these labels—to hide behind it. Paresh Som probably meant something of the sort by mentioning narrowing down the area. One has to deal with a large canvas when one talks about economic capability; the terms 'conservative', 'communist', 'bourgeoise' or 'reactionary' are relatively safe.

Aditya knows all these are meaningless arguments. Tiring. They don't get you anywhere. They probably would if he was a political person primarily and then a writer. Since he's not so and never was, there's no point in paying heed to what people think or say about him. If he has any accountability, it's to himself, to his conscience.

Lunchtime is almost over by the time he calls Chitra and dictates three letters or so. It's not fair to delay her any longer.

Adiya says, "Enough for now. We'll do the rest after lunch."

"Are you going out?"

"No."

It is quite sunny now. The sun is so strong that the beige walls appear white. Who'll say that it rained so heavily just a while ago! The ray of sunlight touches Chitra's face and body and reaches the steel almirah behind her. It would have been hot if the air-conditioner wasn't turned on.

The job is done for the time being, but since Chitra waits with her eyes on the shorthand notebook, Aditya asks, "Want to say something?"

"Can I leave a little early today? About three-thirty, four o'clock?"

"Why?" Aditya asks, "Personal work?"

"No", Chitra hesitates. Pushing behind a lock of her shampooed hair falling on her forehead, Chitra says "There was a lot of tension in the locality last night. The police had come to comb the area. They're anticipating more disturbances today—"

"There are disturbances all around. It's a daily affair—" Aditya ruminates on the draft of the Managing Director's speech. If Chitra leaves early, he can't complete the job by this evening. He says, "You'll go to Bhowanipore. That's a relatively safe area."

"I don't live in Bhowanipore any more."

Chitra looks straight at Aditya. The side of her face turned to the sun is flushed. "I have been in Baranagar for a month", Chitra says, "at my mother's."

"Oh. You didn't tell me."

"What's there to tell? You know everything."

Lowering her eyes, Chitra rubs the pencil on her lips. Her face is still a little flushed. Her hairstyle has changed. The subject is personal. Thought he knows the background, any further curiosity would be uncalled for. Chitra might feel that Aditya is taking advantage of his position.

"Alright. You can definitely go if you have a problem."

"I'll do these letters immediately." She stands up as soon as he replies, "Any other urgent work too."

"Didn't I give a draft to be typed?"

"It's almost done."

"Okay. Send that in after lunch."

Aditya draws the curtains after Chitra leaves. With the change in light, the familiar room looks new. The chairs, table, table lamp, books on the shelf, steel almirah, the calendar on the wall look different. They way one's own bedroom appears different after a three-hour nap on a Sunday afternoon. The mind gets a little alienated. The three hours in between seem to be all important—maybe the most crucial thing in life. So many things could have been done. One can't of course recall what. Trying to remember is even more depressing. The heart aches, the head seems dull, the tea seems tasteless. One has to slump in the chair looking at the sky–waiting for the sky to turn darker. At one point of time, the darkness becomes most desirable. One gets the feeling that life, survival, relationship all have a monotonous routine, not so much of a fulfilment. This may not be only his feeling, many others must have felt the same way. After carrying on with this daily living, people keep walking, simply because there is a road to walk on. Even though, there's no certain address, no definite destination to reach. One can't declare this terrible experience. Then one has to stop. And to stop is to hold the cold pistol butt on one's own head. One begins to cheat oneself to hide one's desperation— trying to kiss one's own cheek.

Aditya spends some more time on such random brooding. Lunchtime is not yet over. He can be on his own now. He can climb down from the second to the first floor and go to the officers' canteen and have a chit-chat. He's a little hungry too. Or, he can even go to the office of the magazine 'Our Times' or to College Street. He can even take an aimless walk down the street—he can walk through the street littered with raw coconut shells, cast-away sal leaves on which peas and potatoes were served, the smell of stale paneer or fried eggs and see the faces of those whom he recognises so well when he sits at his writing table.

Aditya doesn't do any of these. At his chair, swayed by loose thoughts, he is caught up with another thought. Actually this is just like him. He has been trapped with responsibilities thrust on him day after day, year after year, his limbs have become numb. His blood doesn't flow—even when he comes out of the trap, he keeps staring at it. This trap is his shelter and his warfield where he continuously differentiates himself from others. In his mind, speed develops; time becomes valuable. If he is dragged out to the road, his feet will become immobile. His nails will be drawn inside his flesh—he won't need to use the nailcutter sitting in the soft sun. He may run—or he'll run when the man next to him is attacked and his own existence becomes precarious. He had run once. After running to sufficient safety, he had got on to a taxi to further security, unhesitatingly stuffed a whole note into the driver's palm because he would have to wait in the street if he wanted the change. Of course, he had phoned the police station after that. Ever since, all his living moments are spent in the hope of finding news of the crime in the morning papers.

There's a knock on the door. He straightens up from his crouching position.

Chitra is back, a sheaf of papers in her hand.

"The letters are done. I've brought them since you are in."

"You were in a hurry, not me. Don't say that you had to miss lunch because of me."

" I didn't say that." Chitra smiles shyly. She steps across the side of the table and places the typed letters in front of Aditya.

"Sit down."

Aditya doesn't show any signs of hurrying up. He observes Chitra sitting down. How old can she be? Twenty-five, twenty-six? Maybe a couple of years more. She can't be called pretty, there's no fault in her features though. Her face has an equal share of charm and intelligence. There's an innocence in her eyes—that innocence turns into embarrassment if one looks straight at her. She betrays how fragile her smartness is.

It would embarrass her if he observed her for long. As he looks down at the table unmindfully, Chitra fidgets with the neckline of her blouse.

"Since you didn't say anything yourself, I didn't want to ask you." Aditya hesitates. "But—"

Chitra looks up.

"What do you want to know? Why I left Bhowanipore?"

"I know the reason." Aditya stops intentionally, he lets Chitra take in the abruptness of the question. And then says, "A relationship, if it breaks once, can't be put together, however hard one tries. A crack remains."

Her teeth are on her lips. She bites her lips so hard that they turn pale. Chitra doesn't reply.

Aditya continues, "You've confided in my wife, I've heard a bit from her. Often, relatives, even parents, provoke conflicts. I felt you could have reconciled if you and Salil had stayed at a distance from others."

Chitra asks, "What's the point in reconciling with someone I don't love, have no respect for?"

"You're saying that out of sentimentality or out of anger. It may not be your real feeling. We excavate many reasons out of our decisions after they have already been taken."

Chitra squirms in her chair, as if she doesn't know what to do with herself.

"I remember your family didn't approve of your marrying Salil. Your father had even tried to go to Court. After all that, can you shirk off responsibility by saying you don't love or respect him! You could have a little more patience."

"Who'll decide on the measure of patience?" Chitra says, "The one who has to suffer or outsiders?"

"That's true, of course." Aditya sounds subdued, "I can't lay down the limit of your patience."

"I didn't say that." Chitra's eyes seem to visualise Aditya in various roles—her boss at office, an acquaintance, and also a well-wisher who has intervened in her life's crises. Composing herself, she says, "I know why you have brought up the topic. My father is no more, Ma had told me to talk to you. Salil has a regard for you, he might have listened to you. But that would only delay the process, nothing would come out of it."

Aditya keeps silent.

"It's so humiliating!" Chitra continues, "A man who has no love for his wife, no respect—who scolds the maid for serving food to his working wife after a full day's office—would he love or respect me at somebody's bidding! What do you say, should I have accepted that?"

It would have relieved her, had she been able to yell out the words, the suppressed tone only aggravated Chitra's uneasiness. What she can't express flows out as drops of tears down her cheeks. She tries to control herself by covering her eyes with her handkerchief which had been tucked at the waist into her saree.

"No, I don't say that." Aidtya doesn't try to console her. "Maybe you've taken the right step. You should do what you really want to. I shouldn't have brought up the topic. Sorry."

"There's nothing to feel sorry about. Only those who are concerned about me talk about it." Chitra smiles at last. An embarrassed smile. She says, "Don't worry about me. I'm okay."

"Good. You should be strong."

Aditya is at a loss for words.

"Salil has asked for divorce. He'll marry somebody else." Chitra takes the initiative now. Says, "There wouldn't have been such a mess if he had come clear. He thought I would create problems for him. Why should I! I don't depend on him!"

Aditya nods in a manner that might mean both yes and no. Looking away from Chitra, he mutters, "I don't know. Maybe that's the way to take it."

"How else can I take it! He's a hypocrite. He was cooking up excuses because he couldn't face up to the fact. He's a coward."

Chitra appears to be repeating herself. Not the way she has said it before. Rather, this time each of her words is loaded with hatred and aggression; window panes seem to be smashed at the assault of pebbles. The target is not Salil, but Aditya. The pieces of glass are piercing Aditya's head. He needs to defend himself—which means that Chitra has to leave.

Aditya busily looks at his watch.

"Goodness! It's pretty late."

"I've wasted your time." Chitra stands up and says, "I've spoken only to you. It's personal. Embarrassing to talk about it. Please don't mind."

Why should I mind! Only that it's difficult to put two and two together."

Memories are congealing into words. Creative writing teaches the proper use of words. The same word can cross boundaries and reach to a larger meaning by the correct usage. The background may change, even incidents. After Chitra leaves, Aditya broods, since the morning till a little while ago, Chitra was nowhere around—even if he had written his diary, Chitra wouldn't have existed in it. Then, why did he have to bother about her problems? Was it because the subject was too heavy for him and he needed self-defence?

The telephone buzzes loudly. He picks up the receiver at the second ring.

"Hello?"

"Mr Ray?"

"Yes."

"Call from your residence."

"Hello."

"Listen, it's me."

Sweta's voice. Almost unexpected. Aditya's brow creases.

"What's up?"

"Listen, after you left for office, someone called twice or thrice."

"What do you mean?"

"I don't know. He was asking whether this number is yours, whether this address is yours."

"Who was it? You didn't ask his name?"

"He didn't leave his name." Sweta's voice sounds agitated. She says, "He hung up as soon as I asked his name. Then a little while ago, some other man called. He didn't give his name either. Asked about your office—"

"Did you tell them say?"

"Yes."

"And then?"

"He has left a number. Wants you to call."

"Strange." Aditya is irritated, "Will the number alone do? You should have asked for his name!"

"Why're you shouting at me?" Sweta says, "He didn't give his name, said the number will do."

Aditya jots down the number as Sweta dictates it and guesses that the exchange is of this area. Maybe some office nearby. It doesn't look like a personal number. Not that there's no residential area in Dalhousie. But, he cannot remember coming across such a number.

Aditya broods as he speaks to Sweta.

"Did the voice seem familiar?"

"No."

"Alright. Let me see." Aditya stops and asks, "Was Pritha at home?"

"Pritha has gone to Ballygunge Gardens, to Sharmistha's. She'll have lunch there—"

"Bacchu's also at school?"

"Yes."

Aditya says, "If any more such calls come, just give my office number. Don't go into anything else."

"Okay." Sweta says, "This has never happened before. It wasn't a wrong number. Can you make out whose number it is?"

"No." Aditya says, "But it may be someone I know. Maybe the line got disconnected accidentally. Calcutta Telephones! Anyway, don't worry. I'll see. Tell Satya not to respond to crank calls."

"When are you coming home?"

"Lets me see."

"Kanchan'll come in the evening. You remember, don't you?"

"Yes." Aditya is trying to end the conversation. "Bye."

A flood of emptiness sweeps in as he hangs up the telephone. As the waves retreat all of a sudden, the wet sand, the dryness of the scene still cling to his eyes. The words ring in his ears—he's a hypocrite, he's a coward! Aditya withdraws, changing the course of his thought, he thinks he's no better than Salil. And then realises, if anyone had called about matters of work, he wouldn't have been so evasive. He would have given his name, introduced himself properly. Sweta can't make a mistake. She said clearly that though the man took his number, he had asked Aditya to call up. It must have struck Sweta before him. Otherwise, she wouldn't have called him at office. Usually, she notes down his phone calls in her head and tells him when he returns.

Who can it be!

Before asking for the number, Aditya holds on to the receiver for some time. Should he go through the PBX? He's confused. There's a direct line in the chamber—he uses that on special purpose or for private conversations. Right now he has a six-digit number in his head, nothing else; there's no name or features associated with the name. It may even be a ghost call. He had read in the papers a few days earlier that ghost calls had gone up recently and complaints about this are pouring in at Telephone Bhavan and newspaper offices. Usually in the afternoon when the master of the house is away, children at schools and colleges and no one but women and young girls are at home—. They call suddenly—maybe waking you up from siesta—and ask strange questions or utter obscene sentences. The callers are usually men, presumably unemployed young men. There was an attempt by the papers at an explanation that, this is nothing but a social disorder. In 1970, there were about 50 lakh unemployed people enrolled in the employment exchange. Ten years earlier, in 1960–61, the figure was 18 lakh. That's the official record. It may be assumed that many don't get themselves enrolled, so the actual figure is larger. Out of this, a big chunk is the educated lot. Fundamentally, while population is growing at the rate of 2.25%, employment is going up at the rate of over 12%. In this unnerving situation, the urban educated youth who don't have a social or economic identity, have no clue to their own future—don't even have any political ideal, many fall prey to mental problems, etc. etc. Maybe, maybe not, Aditya doesn't know. He feels at times straightforward explanations like these too have some problems, trying to evade the real issue by spinning words.

Dialling the direct line, he gets an engaged sound. It's ringing intermittently in a monotonous note, almost as if it is recorded. It's irritating. Aditya gives up at the third attempt. It may also be that the line itself is faulty even though the dial tone is there, it's probably unable to connect properly. Sweta too spoke through the operator.

But is there really the need for all this urgency? The caller wanted Aditya, not the other way round. If there is an urgency, it's that person's. Not going into all these problems, if he has any responsibility to the caller, Aditya can give the number to the operator, if the line can be connected, well and good otherwise he'll forget all about it. Besides, he does not need to be all that secretive about an unknown number that he has to call on the direct line. He's probably giving more importance to the episode than is due to it.

Not getting any clue from the various possibilities, Aditya yells in silence—who can it be? He doesn't get an answer. He gives the number to the operator with the instruction to give the line to him as soon as it is connected. He returns to the continuity of uneasiness. There's no definite picture to his thoughts now.

As it happens in a film where various, apparently disjointed, scenes are tied into a montage, almost like that— it's an evening, he and Salil sitting on the balcony of their Wood Street flat, Sweta and Pritha with Chitra opposite them; four youths lined up on Beleghata canalside in the early dawn; Benoy Hazra's face, a tall and thin man running from west to east of the Maidan; another man running towards Theatre Road almost in the dark; Chitra shouts, he's a hypocrite, he's a coward—

The telephone. He picks up the receiver promptly and says, "Hello" when the operator says, "Speak. Your number is responding."

"Hello?"

"Yes."

Collecting himself, Aditya asks, "Whose number is this?"

"Intelligence Branch. Lalbazar." The same voice replies. "Whom do you want?"

He sits up at the mention of Intelligence Branch but he feels a needle of doubt. He says in a controlled manner, "My name is Aditya Ray. A message was given to my flat at Wood Street that I was to telephone this number. What's the matter?"

"Oh, hold on—"

As he waits, he can hear a faint voice on the other side, Sarkar, take it quick, it's your case, Aditya Ray—it becomes inaudible after that. In a few seconds, another voice comes on the line, "Hello."

"I'm Aditya Ray speaking."

"Mr Ray? Good afternoon Sir."

"Yes. Tell me."

"Are you the writer Aditya Ray?"

"If you're from the IB, you must have all the

information." In a stern and impatient voice, Aditya asks, "Who is speaking?"

"You want to know my name? Sarkar—"

"Yes. Tell me."

"It's about your diary." The man who introduced himself as Sarkar takes time. Aditya keeps the receiver down and picks it up again. He says, "You gave information at Park Street Police Station on 5th morning—you had seen something at Maidan."

"Yes. A man was shot dead. Murdered."

Aditya falls silent.

Sarkar continues, "You had informed over the telephone. You didn't sign on the diary."

"I'll sign if needed."

"Mr Ray, let me speak, please."

"Okay, go on."

"We have investigated the case on the basis of your words. After all, you are a known personality. But, Sir, we didn't get anything in the investigation."

"What do you mean?" Aditya gets excited.

Sarkar clears his throat. Says, "Nothing of the sort happened on that day. Your information is incorrect."

"What the hell are you saying? Did I lie? I saw it with my own eyes—"

Sarkar doesn't let him complete. He says, "You may be mistaken. Besides, you're an important person—we need your co-operation. If you too give such fictitious—"

"What! You say its fictitious!" Blood rushes to Aditya's head. Moving the receiver to the other hand, he says, "I should have known that there's no point in telling the police. Because it's the police who committed the murder. Like you've done at Beleghata, at Baranagar, at—"

"You're quoting newspaper reports. Anyway, I've informed you of our report. If you have anything more to say, Sir, you may go to the DC. We're closing the case."

The dial tone returns. They've disconnected the line. They began on a polite note and ended by being rude. Which means it doesn't matter what Aditya makes of this.

Aditya sits shellshocked for some time. The bearer has already brought the afternoon tea—he remembers he was having the heated conversation over the phone then. He takes one sip and keeps the cup aside. His taste buds have gone numb. His hands are trembling. The room is cool, but he's sweating at his neck and brow. He wipes his forehead with his bare hands. It seems, even though that man referred to him as a known personality more than once, he had a tendency to reduce him to a non-entity. He didn't even hesitate to say that the incident as reported by Aditya is fictitous. Pondering over the entire dialogue, Aditya realises that the man had not acknowledged the happening of the incident. He seemed to have the explicit intention of insulting him. Was it to scare him? Can't be sure. But whatever the intention was; the one who spoke, the man who called himself Sarkar— he must have realised Aditya was not one to give up easily. But Aditya immediately realises, what's that to the police? This man is in the Intelligence Branch or a representative of the police. In the same position, a Mukherjee or Banerjee or

Mitra or Chowdhury would have spoken in the same way. But, he, Aditya Ray, nothing but an individual—representing himself and all alone; he's not a part of a group. The police won't take him seriously.

Before he hung up, the man had said he was closing the case. Does that mean that there's no punishment for a crime, not even a protest? Looking at it logically, taking it as a closed case, his responsibility too is over. He can justify to himself that he has fulfilled his responsibility by informing the police. But in a society in which the administration can label a witnessed murder fictitious, what more responsibility can he fulfil! Four days have passed since. If he becomes vocal after four days, it'll not be acceptable to many—it may really seem imaginary.

Faced with all these questions and answers, Aditya feels lost. But the anger is not subsiding—he has to do something but doesn't know what, a smoke of helplessness engulfs him. The incident may get its importance if he starts all over again. Maybe this telephone conversation has the seeds of a new beginning. He may not take it as an end what the police considers as closed. Rather, as a citizen of a democratic state, he can lodge a complaint against the police for harassing him and his wife. The man had said he could go to the DC if he wanted. He can, of course. Even in writing. He can also write to the Press. He'll be criticised for reacting late; but nobody can say that Aditya Ray is building up a fictitious incident to fight against the police. The problem is that he's an intellectual. The stand of the police is quite clear from the threat. Your telephone report of the murder is of no consequence; but the report was made known to you because you're an important person. Don't expect anything more, now keep shut!

Aditya can't make up his mind even after analysing all the angles. He suddenly remembers Ashok Dutta. Ashok too is in the police. He had thought about telling him the day of the incident, he had ultimately decided against it. He could advise him as a friend. He can also find out who this Sarkar fellow is.

His personal telephone book has Ashok's number. He pulls his attaché towards himself to take it out. Chitra returns, with some papers.

As he opens the attaché to look for the telephone book, Aditya asks, "What's up? you haven't left yet?"

"I was supposed to get the draft ready!"

"It's done?"

"Yes."

"Alright. Leave it. I'll have a look at it later." Aditya forces a smile. "Thank you."

His calculations go wrong at times. Even a familiar road ends in a blind lane—can't find the way out. Aditya is in two minds, even after finding Ashok's number. Though he's a friend, who knows what role Ashok'll take. He had spoken about his cousin a few days earlier; he couldn't try to locate his own cousin in spite of his position. He might try to evade Aditya's problem despite the personal relationship. Besides, the question is of morals, not of arguments. If Ashok tells him to withdraw, he can do that, because the murder doesn't have anything to do with his own survival. But should Aditya prevent himself from doing anything about it? If not, then, why involve Ashok in it? Or, as the hurt attenuates, is Aditya looking for a support in self-defence? Is he getting trapped in apprehensions? He doesn't have the strength to go ahead with his moral stand?

No, there's no point involving Ashok in all this. It's not impossible that Ashok has already heard about it and he's deliberately avoiding him.

The worries are not taking him anywhere. Rather, with time, they are trapping him in the same groove. An uneasy feeling is spreading all over his body. If he were dissected, his flesh-blood-brain-breath would have nothing but worries of different shapes and shades. All alone within himself—a complete world within himself. There's no one else in that world, or if there are, they all have Aditya's features. The same age, hunched with the weight of time and conscience, chasing one another, as if in a musical chair, tense about self-defence when the signal for stopping comes. No incidents occur, but even if they do not in the normal sequence—they rise up or climb down, move forward or backward as if to weave a spider's net. Everything happens mechanically. There's a clash but it doesn't scratch the body—it comes in a different voice over the telephone. The ego about one's internationalism acquired through books and newspapers are boosted—one signs quickly the protest letters on Vietnam and Bangladesh. Nothing more, nothing else.

There's no comfort in such thoughts about oneself. In spite of it, this evening, Aditya thinks about himself this way. He gets out of the office for a change.

The streets are already jammed. He looks at the sky before getting into the car. After sunset, the clouds are forming again. It's not stuffy. Humid cool breeze. A deep breath lightens his head. He sits at the back and rolls down both windows. He looks out. It's not the end of office time yet, but the crowd on the road gives the impression that the office hours are over—all going towards their respective places alone or in a group. Chitra can't be found in this crowd. The girl left almost half an hour back. Strange! One who calls someone a coward for being dishonest and who is not fragile even at the breakdown of marriage, what longing for security urges her to go home early!

He had told Abdul to drive towards College Street. Aditya changes his mind after crossing Writers and Lalbazar. He instructs the car to turn to the right. He had promised Debu Chowdhury to see him at the office of "Our Times". He's free today, he can go there.

The office is on the first floor. Debu Chowdhury is in his room. He comes forward and ushers Aditya to a chair. As he moves to his seat, he asks, "Have you come to the newspaper office or to meet me?"

"To be honest, neither." Aditya has calmed himself down although the worries linger in his mind. He smiles and says, "I was getting bored in office. So I got out. I wanted to go to College Street. Then I decided to see you—"

"Good." Debu Chowdhury orders the bearer to get coffee. And then says, "Good that you didn't go to College Street. It's closed today."

"Why?"

"Anticipating problems. Some Naxalite leader has been arrested."

"Do you know who?"

"How do I know? The reporters are on the move. There's no confirmation yet. You can tap the news department when you go. You might get some news there."

There's no reason to it but Aditya feels depressed. The large chunk of the sky can be seen from the window, three strokes of electric current flash across the clouds. The clouds are darker and thicker now than when he left office—the gaps in the sky are getting filled up. As he gazes out, the sound of the ceiling fan jars in his ears.

"This was bound to happen," Debu Chowdhury says, "We've created this situation through our misdeeds over the last twenty-three, twenty-four years. The leaders should have been careful if they had any idea of the fallout of their doings. It's not clear for whom this independent democratic India is meant. If you see the economic and social disparities, it appears there's a dependent country within the independent one. The idea about total freedom is lost—"

Photographs of Rabindranath and Gandhi hang behind Debu Chowdhury. Under the glass of the table, there is a Viswa Bharati print of *Where the Mind is Without Fear*. The memories of a universe now past and with which today's reality has no touch.

Many people talk like Debu Chowdhury. They did yesterday, maybe they'll do so tomorrow. If you keep your ears pricked it will seem to you that the same essay on society, politics, economics has been torn into pieces of various sizes and handed over to all—each one is reciting his own piece with no cue. The speeches do not give away any distinctiveness. The same face is forced on a tall or a short, a thin or a fat, a fair or a dark body. For some differentiation, a pair of glasses or a cigar or shining teeth are loaned. The rapid and much-repeated words from the quotations look as if they are meant to be used in certificates in theatre ads—there's no expression of original thoughts.

"Frustration gives birth to the desire to disown—" Debu Chowdhury continues in the midst of Aditya's absent-mindedness. He picks a cigar from a square flat colourful tin case and lights it. The odour of cigar floats around. Holding the cigar between his fingers, he says, "Whatever is happening, nothing is natural."

Aditya silently sips his coffee. He's still aware of his worries in spite of coming out of his own four walls. Probably because of the cigar smell, his taste buds are growing numb. The coffee fails to invigorate him.

"Why were you looking for me?"

"About your story 'The Other Side of the Reflection'. Brilliant. I read it after it was composed. And then I thought let me discuss it before printing."

"What's the problem?"

"Nothing major." Debu Chowdhury hesitates, "It's an extraordinary story. But the subject is somewhat risky. Times are bad. I hope you don't fall into trouble over it."

Aditya is startled. He stares at Debu Chowdhury for a while and says, "It's a simple story about a father and son conflict. After a point of time, the son finds his own honest father a cheat. He reacts. Why should I fall in trouble because of this?"

"Political stories are not written much in this country. From that angle, this story is fascinating. But—"

Debu Chowdhury looks worried. Keeping quiet for a little while, he continues, "I felt the story's a little biased. There's an accusation. If it's misinterpreted, you and I will be pulled up. We might be taken as instigators. Congress at the Centre, President's Rule here. The police are up in arms. You know all political problems are now tackled by the Detective Department. Everyone is criminals in their eyes."

Noticing Aditya's silence, Debu Chowdhury too pauses. Pondering over his next sentence, he says, "See what happened to our friend Subandhu Mitra's story 'The Assassin's Administration'. The police have arrested him. He'll be released, I hear. But they haven't as yet. That was also a simple factual report."

As he listens, the old pain returns to Aditya. His jaws stiffen. He says, "Debuda, I don't believe in speculation with writing. I have a limited ambition—that is to remain honest to myself, nothing more than that—"

Debu Chowdhury snatches at his words. He says, "None but a scoundrel can call you dishonest."

Aditya feels Debu Chowdhury is obsessed with his own words. Otherwise he needn't have said this now.

"I didn't say that", Trying to come back to the point, Aditya says, "As a writer, I won't go down the streets with a rifle to protest against wrongs; I don't want to be applauded for raising slogans on class struggle. You know I'm not a member of any political party—Congress, Communist or Naxalite. So there's no question of any bias. But, I'll write what I see, what I feel. You call that bias, accusation. I think any conscientious person would do the same."

"I understand. I said the story is terrific. But stuff like this can be written when the times are a little cooler, isn't it? If it's printed now, nobody would bother about its literary value; they'll think otherwise."

Aditya doesn't have a reply immediately. Not that he takes time to think; uneasiness is apparent on his face. After keeping silent for a while, he asks "What do you suggest?"

"Why don't you brush up the story a little?" Debu Chowdhury says, "Leaving out the pain ant the sarcasm, it won't harm the artistic value of the story—"

A suppressed smile breaks on Aditya's face. He's feeling hot. He pulls off the tie and folding it, says, "So you too are scared?"

"I'm not scared for myself. For the paper. It would be a different matter if it was a party paper. It's true we don't value business over quality but this is a commercial paper. Government advertisements have stopped after Subandhu Mitra's piece was carried. If the publication itself has to close down for some reason? However much we shout about democracy, we don't have the guts to accept political opposition, criticism, and so on."

Aditya tries to judge how serious Debu Chowdhury is. The doubt is natural, there's no mistake in the context. He suddenly remembers, the day before he left for Bombay, the Managing Director Mahadevan had called him to say that the profiles in terms of age, education, sex, income of readers of the newspapers carrying their advertisements are known readership surveys. But the profiles of the newspapers are not known. Without being a party paper, a particular newspaper may turn out to be dangerous for its political opinion. Some information about this needs to be recorded. Although he didn't say it explicitly, Aditya now feels, the matter is not so simple. Debu Chowdhury too possibly means something of the sort.

Self-justification sometimes becomes problematic. The solution of the present problem is to withdraw the story without further conversation. But, given his relationship with Debu Chowdhury, that would be impoliteness. For twenty years or more, this man has never rejected him. He has argued with him, criticised him but he has been supportive. Debu Chowdhury is no Dhruva Nandi.

With as much intimacy as he can garner, Aditya says, "Is there really any reason to be so scared? Administration gets crazy when pushed to the walls. But in India or West Bengal, it's wrong to assume that fascism has arrived. Maybe it's on its way, I don't know. But why would we be scared and support fascism ourselves?"

Debu Chowdhury crouches in his chair with a depressed look. He doesn't reply.

Aditya says, "You've done a lot for me, I won't create problems. Give me back the story."

"Now you're getting angry." Debu Chowdhury says, "I have certain right over you. I won't return it just like that."

"But you won't carry it."

"Let me see. Let me consider a little more. If I can take the risk."

Debu Chowdhury leans back. The worried face seems to relax. It's not possible to make out how it is forced. He opens the cigar case and holds it out to Aditya—knowing that Aditya is not a smoker, he picks one himself.

"Will you have one?"

"I don't smoke." Aditya tries to relax himself. He smiles and says, "But let me smoke today."

Aditya picks up a cigar. He wonders whether he can confide in Debu Chowdhury. Anything told in a newspaper office spreads like wildfire. The incident will be taken as such—nobody will care about the tension that Aditya Ray has gone through because of this. It may also be misinterpreted. It's better to wait. The incident which has kept itself wrapped up for four days, won't get dusty very soon. As he lights up the cigar with the match-stick held by Debu Chowdhury, Aditya realises, since the afternoon, as he is moving towards a decision, his language is getting tougher. In the darkness of his thoughts, words are becoming active, the words are brushing off the dust and putting on their war clothes as if on a sudden instruction. They have no idea what that war is like, what the future is. The curiosity to know is gradually getting exhausted. The aim is just one, and that is to explode louder than bullets. To know and to expose.

As he puffs on the cigar, Aditya chokes from lack of habit. He coughs and exhales smoke desperately. He tries to smile.

Debu Chowdhury watches him in surprise.

"Throw it away if it doesn't suit you. These things take time to get accustomed to."

Aditya clears his throat and prepares to puff again.

"Taking time is an excuse. The real thing is to get used to the uneasiness."

"Any way," Debu Chowdhury changes track, not getting what Aditya means, "Your daughter's college hasn't opened yet?"

Aditya shakes his head.

"No. No news when it will. The girl is getting tense."

"Why!"

"Their group has got dispersed. Many of her friends are missing. She pounces on the morning newspaper for news of murders and arrests. I know she looks for names. She turns pale at the noise of police vans at night. Who'll tell her this is nothing new—the noise was always there, always will be."

In the midst of the conversation, silence ensues. Aditya glances out to see it getting dark. Maybe because of the clouds. The clouds have turned dark. He looks at the watch and prepares to leave. Sweta had reminded him that Kanchan was expected. Although he has the car with him, the roads are jammed at this time. The saving grace is that his house is not too far.

"Right, we can't appreciate their tension." Debu Chowdhury says, "I don't know where this Naxalbari will lead to. So much being said—social menace, romanticism, adventurism and what not. Many whom the police have arrested or killed have criminal records. Not impossible. Lumpens take advantage of all situations, many a time they are hired on purpose. But, who can deny that in the last four-five years, a generation of our best boys has been destroyed. If they didn't dream of a revolution, they could have completed their studies, taken up jobs and got established quite easily. Just imagine what potential each one had. Whether right or wrong, what tremendous courage, sacrifice! The country will miss them one day. People will realise—"

Aditya knows he is not wrong. Privately, when he argues in his mind, he thinks the same way. But, when someone else articulates, it sounds like a speech—the words seem to lead to self-betrayal. The body aches. The honesty of emotions flies off like bits of torn paper.

Debu Chowdhury looks so excited, he would probably carry on. Somebody pushes the door and walks in.

"Debnarayan Chowdhury?"

"Yes. It's me. What is it?"

"Good evening."

Aditya turns to see a man step inside the room and stop abruptly. Not more than thirty-five. Neither tall, nor short, neither thin nor fat—a non-descript face. Terribly fair, sharp features which go well with the thin gold-rimmed glasses. Cropped beard. Meticulously clean dhoti-kurta and a sling bag on the shoulder gives an aristocratic look—next-door neighbour to Derozio or Keshav Sen. But the voice is effeminate. Slight stammer. The Good Evening sounds like 'Good Vening.'

Not getting any response from Debu Chowdhury, he introduces himself in his feminine voice:

"I'm Rangan Sengupta. I had brought an article—"

"What article?"

He pulls out a rolled-up bunch of papers from the sling bag and hands it over.

Debu Chowdhury takes the manuscript. He glances through and his brow creases. He says, "The Music of the Wasted Youth". What does that mean? What's the subject of the article?"

"It's about youth power. Its influence on the cultural, political life in France, Latin America, Indonesia, a synthesis of all that."

"Where's the synthesis?" Debu Chowdhury sounds disgusted, "This is a thesis. Almost a book. Where do we have so much space?"

Aditya knows the young man will continue and Debu Chowdhury will get irritated. They are uneasy in his presence. It's time for him to leave.

"I'll make a move. I'll come some other day."

"Yes, it's tough to sit through this." Debu Chowdhury asks, "Where'll you go now? Straight home?"

"I'll peep into the newsroom. Will Pradipta be there?"

"He is usually there at his time."

"Okay."

He doesn't have to go up to the newsroom. Before that, he meets Pradipta Mukherjee. A craze as a political correspondent. His brisk walk gives away that he's going out. Aditya stops.

"I was going to see you."

"You always say that when we meet." Pradipta reaches out to him. "Famous writer, senior executive—why'll you remember us?"

"You're joking." Aditya says, "You seem to be in a hurry."

"I have to go to Writers. From there to Lalbazar. I'll get back and file the report. We're always in a hurry."

Pradipta holds his hand, "How are you? Haven't seen you for a long time."

"Famous writer. Senior executive!"

Both burst out laughing.

Praditpta looks at his watch, "Did you really come to see me?"

"Yes. I had come to see Debu. I thought I'll see you too." Pradipta's eye balls are invisible through his thick glasses. Trying to look at his eyes, Aditya's vision gets blocked by the glasses. He asks, "Heard some big leader has been arrested?"

"Yes. Saibal Majumdar."

"Who?"

"Saibal Majumdar. Secretary to the State Committee."

Seeing that Aditya is unable to comprehend, Pradipta says, "Don't you remember? Veteran journalist, he used to come to the Press Club regularly once. Tall, thin—he would crouch a little while walking. You must have seen him—"

Cigar smoke is choking him, his voice is getting trapped inside. Gulping down the smoke, Aditya asks, "When?"

"Can't say yet. The news came as a surprise. The police

are not giving it out. I'm running around for this. Let's see if I can get some details for tomorrrow's issue. I hear they arrested him at some hideout in South Calcutta—"

Aditya listens with his eyes to the floor. He keeps quiet.

"Will you go anywhere else or return home?"

"No." Aditya says, "Let's make a move."

They walk side by side. The staircase across the passage. Vintage building. Aditya has been seeing it almost from his birth. The echo of their footsteps numbs memories. Aditya knows Pradipta's mind is on a different track. But the sound of footsteps are both of theirs.

"If the report is correct, it'll be a setback for the Marxist-Leninist movement." Pradipta comments as they walk down. "As it is, in-fighting within the group is heightening. Many are now against Charu Majumdar. Saibalda had a large following among the urban youth."

Pradipta stops on the pavement. Aditya stops too. The drizzle touches them and Aditya looks up. It's pitch dark. Threatening to be torrential.

"How's your writing"?

"So-so." Aditya says, "Hard to get motivated."

"Why?"

Aditya doesn't reply.

Pradipta signals at the car with the 'Press' label, waiting at a distance. And says, "I read your novel 'Conflict'. Powerful novel."

Aditya smiles.

Pradipta says, "But is it enough to write fiction now? Write other things."

"What other things?"

"About this time—what's happening all around. Why don't the intellectuals react?"

"Maybe they do. But who'll print them?"

"Give our daily. We'll carry them to. We're thinking of starting an open forum called The Other View."

"Let me see. I'll be in touch with you if I do write."

"Come another day. We'll have a chat." Pradipta's car has been driven forward. Opening the door and stepping in, he says, "Don't forget the article."

Aditya waves in consent.

Burnt mobile smell along with rain. The net of smoke in his throat. Aditya tries to take a deep breath. He intends to go home but is standing on the pavement in the drizzle, Aditya thinks, a conscientious man can't have home as the only destination. All the other relationships build up a structure which is an unreal picture of the country, the times. Maybe Pradipta was right, why doesn't he react?

He had bought a paan to get rid of the nausea. As he munches on it, he tells Abdul, "Don't take Park Street. Take Chowringhee."

"You won't go home, Sir?"

"I will. You take Chowringhee."

It's dark inside the car. Yet, Abdul is trying to look at him in the mirror. A faint view of the chin, a portion of the ear. One can't recognise anyone from this unless he's very familiar. Even that gets fuzzy with headlight of the car behind. As the car passes by, he realises his image has vanished from the mirror. Abdul's forehead and eye have taken its place. Aditya ruminates on Pradipta's description of the man, many of his acquaintances are thin and tall, they may even have a slouching gait. But, no, even though he has heard the name of Saibal Majumdar, he doesn't know him. He would have remembered otherwise.

The rain splashes inside the car. Although the wiper needs to be put on, Aditya doesn't pull up the window on his side. The rain lashing against him, he keenly looks to his right. The hazy Maidan, the fluorescent bulbs are visible through the rain, the front of the Victoria, the headlights of numerous cars on the west of the Red Road. It's nothing like the darkness of that day. The darkness of the evening and that of dawn are not comparable. The difference enabled him to make out that van, that man and the other men. The man must have been wearing white or else he wouldn't have been visible in the dark. He would have been more visible even if the bullets were not shot. But then, he would have known more.

"Abdul, take Theatre Road."

"Home?"

"Yes."

They take the same road to Wood Street. Had he noted the taxi number, he could have strengthened the incident about his escaping. But the point is, there was no logic for his taking a taxi then. He was scared.

Kanchan opens the door. Pritha behind him.

"Welcome Adityada. Just a second." Before Aditya realises, the flashbulbs click. Removing the camera from his eyes, Kanchan says, "Now come in, please."

"Whatever you earn, you blow up clicking useless photographs." Aditya pretends to be annoyed. "Now we'll have to stop you from entering the house with the camera."

Kanchan is embarrassed. He scratches his head, "Don't get angry, Sir. I'll ask for your comment when I present the family album. Not before that—"

"Let's see." Aditya asks, "How long are you here?"

"Half an hour."

Pritha takes the attaché from him.

"Why are you so late, Baba?"

"Am I late? Maybe a little. I went to see Debu Chowdhury." Aditya looks around. "Where's Bacchu? And your mother?"

"Bacchu's studying. Ma must be in the bathroom."

"Sit down, Kanchan. I have to talk to you."

Aditya peeps in Bachchu's room. The pressure cooker is whistling in the kitchen. Aroma of mutton being cooked in the air. He takes a deep breath, the sound of rain grows louder. Sweta is combing her hair in front of the mirror. She looks a bit disoriented. She's holding the ribbon between her teeth. She turns around when she sees Aditya's image in the mirror.

"Oh it's you?"

"Were there any more phone calls?"

"No." Sweta pulls her saree over her shoulder. She sounds worried. "Could you make out who it was?"

"Not really."

Sweta looks at him to comprehend. His distracted look

is nothing unusual but he seems different today. He's changing in a hurry. Handing over his kurta-pyjama, Sweta says, "Nuisance to have a telephone at home."

"Can't do without it. Just calculate, almost three-fourth of our connection with the outside world is through the telephone."

"Even then."

Sweta can't find any logic. Going towards the toilet, Aditya says, "Can I have tea?"

Taking a bath and changing doesn't take him long. He feels fresh. The body does not generate self-confidence but there must be a connection. The thoughts fall into place. The text of the letter gets structured in his mind—it won't be difficult to build up the argument. Then sending it to the newspaper and waiting. Watching. It's not certain what'll happen then. But the weight may be unloaded.

The sound of laughter floats up from the drawing room. Kanchan must be playing the fool. Seeing Aditya, Kanchan hides something like an envelope. He looks innocently at the wall.

Aditya asks, "What's the suspense?"

Sweta moves away suppressing a smile. Maybe to get tea.

Aditya casually looks towards the balcony. Although not heavily as before, it's still raining. Wet breeze along with that of the fan. He had heard the music from the bedroom. Dim-dum-dumadam-Jazz. This must be the silly rock of Paresh Som. He must understand it one day. The Rajgherias of the opposite flat left for London some days back. Their son would be alone, they were asked to keep an eye on him. That hasn't been needed though. The fellow has been having a great time in the evenings with his friends—playing records on full volume. Satya said they drink too. Possible. The way they've started, looks as if it will go on for quite some time. Wood Street is not really Calcutta.

"Whose snaps?"

"Ma's." Pritha says, "Not the ordinary type. He has blown them up. Horrible."

"That's really unfair. Not horrible." Kanchan brings forward the envelope hidden behind his back and displays the contents to Aditya. "See, does it look bad?"

Aditya picks up the print. He holds it in front of his eyes.

Sweta returns with two cups of tea. Keeping down the cups on the table, she says, "See how ugly it is. The nostrils look like tumblers—the pores on the skin like pimples."

"The blow-up may turn you into the opposite of what you are." Aditya says, "Mine would probably turn out to be the same. Right, Kanchan?"

"That's true." Kanchan agrees, "But this hasn't yet been retouched. The defects won't be there after retouch."

"Maybe. But the faults once spotted don't disappear however much you retouch. Camera is a stubborn object. It's not your fault."

"Baba, you're a spoilsport." Pritha says, "Got a chance to hook Kanchan Uncle after a long time."

"Do it another day. I won't be present if I'm told in advance."

Aditya's comment is loaded. It means he's trying to stop the conversation, maybe he has to talk to Kanchan.

Sweta gets the message and gets up. Pritha follows. As she leaves, she says, "Your tea is getting cold."

Kanchan puts the photograph in the envelope and keeps it aside. The camera too. Sitting down with the cup of tea, he asks, "Heard the news today?"

"What?"

"I went to the Coffee House. Heard some top Naxalite leader has been arrested. The police couldn't identify him. So he has been released."

Aditya sits grimly.

"Yes, Saibal Majumdar. But I don't know if he has been released.

Chapter 4

The midnight rain makes one very lonely. The monotonous sound of the rain has a kind of hollowness—the bridge between memories and the future changes places, it gets lost with no trace. No crossing over. No going forward and returning. When you suddenly come out of your sleep, you feel like an island, as if you were the last surviving man, living with water-fed memories. Don't take this as good fortune. The invisible wish is terrible. It's approaching, be prepared for its appearance. Emptiness has no timing, there's no certainty when it'll appear, take hold of you, stop your breath abruptly. This moment is important. You decide who you are, what has been your intention so long—what possibility or faith gave you shelter in the rains, wrapped you up with care in winter? When you were like the dry wood standing under the hot sun, then who was it who poured the soothing water? These questions are meant to make you mute. The emptiness gives birth to a sense of suicidal helplessness. Then another picture rises in front of the eyes. In the world filled with dreams, experiences, relations, an accused wakes up and bathes to be taken to the scaffold. Even after losing senses hate keeps him alive. He thinks neither of life nor of death. He knows, life has left him long ago, now death too is leaving him. This is the best time to enjoy his breath!

Aditya wakes up once in the middle of the night to find it raining. The end of the rainy season, it would continue to pour like this. He still realises, for no definite reason, some abstract thoughts are getting hold of him. Like many other things, he doesn't know why this is happening. He looks at his watch, it's half-past three. He takes a round of the dark flat to gauge his own security. Everything is as it should be. Pritha turns in her sleep. Bachchu's breathing can be made out in the dark. Sweta is breathing happily in her sleep. Keeping his ears and eyes open to all these, his body stiffens, also the memories controlled for so long. Is his security then connected with these three human beings, along with the doors, windows, walls, furniture, curtains— apparently helpless, but peacefully sleeping, assuming that everything is alright, passing away the hours in darkness in the hope that the morning will normalise everything! Or, is it that security has no link to hope— reality and the long-standing relationship with a sense of security. The sense provides a shelter, the most secure place, for breathing. Vision, smell and emotions enable him to know Sweta, Pritha, Bachchu or even his own immediate surroundings in the same way that they know him. Lack of habit distances those beyond his abode—even though the eyes know them, these relationships are devoid of emotions.

Maybe, maybe not. The thoughts are not getting

coherent and complete, that is why depression has taken hold of his body. Aditya can't make out where he is, and why! Trying to pull himself out of the discontinuity of memories, he broods, if now, standing like this—when all the others are asleep, something happens to him, he falls flat like the dead furniture, then, when they discover him tomorrow morning, what emptiness will engulf them? It's true, Pritha's feeling won't be the same as Sweta's or Bachchu's. Bachchu is young, he'll borrow experience from Sweta and Pritha to form ideas. Disbelief will keep them mum. For self-defence, one will rush to the other.

Aditya moves back. It can also be that nothing will happen the way he is mentally organising the incidents and feelings. That down when the man ran towards him, he felt one way about the helpless person and about his duty in such circumstances—even after the incident happened, what he considered his responsibility— but when the man actually fell down, throwing all his earlier ideas to the wind, he himself ran for self-defence. Why!

There's no answer. Passing some more time in the uneasy lack of comprehension, he returns to bed. Not exactly to sleep. It's not yet dawn. Maybe another hour and a half or more. Middle of August; the nights have already grown longer, the sky remains dark due to rain and cloud. The way it's raining today, who knows when dawn will break. Besides, if it continues this way, one can't go for a morning walk. The newspapers may also be late.

With the anxiety, his breathing grows heavy. Although it's been some time that he has looked up, his eyes are still hurting. He's not bleary any more. The blades of the slowly rotating ceiling fan can be identified individually, some sounds float even in the silence. Sweta breathing intermittently. In the sudden flash of lightning through the window, her body is visible for a brief while and then is lost. As he unmindfully identifies these sounds and sights, Aditya anticipates that up to this day, everything has followed an order, but a little later, with the break of dawn, when the newspaper hawkers start their morning duty, cycling around over the city, things won't be the same any more.

Last evening when he handed over the letter to Pradipta, he had read it breathlessly and said, "You can kill people, I met you yesterday, you didn't utter a word. How could you keep a sensation like this to yourself?"

Aditya had smiled in silence. There's no reply to straight questions like these. He couldn't have explained to Pradipta that though the letter was a two-page one, the five-day old incident—with which he alone was involved—could have made a complete novel. If there's any continuity between the plan to murder and the actual murder, then the witness to that murder and the wiping of the memories and conscience also have a link between themselves. Though he doesn't know the end of the story, the letter has somehow saved him. He has no idea, the concern for self-defence would probably lead him to suicide. One death would lead to another—in silence and solitude. All deaths don't require the darkness of the Maidan, or the sound of bullets.

The scene is returning to him. In the same sequence as it happened, the way he scripted it. Aditya broods, just as a story is born. The difference is only that there's no beginning, no end. But like in a story, there's a march ahead. He realises he's no longer the person he was before writing the letter and handling it over. In fact, his position would further change after it gets printed. Once the bleeding stops, the bruise glares with the depth of the hurt—instead of the pain, a numb sensation engulfs the feeling. He may feel light, easy after sharing his experience.

Aditya covers his eyes with his hand, drowsy. He yawns—he can't prevent himself from being noisy. Yawning in the darkness of the room and to the sound of rain outside, he senses the touch of a bangled arm on his chest. The hand, after resting on his chest for a while, moves over his neck, brow and head. It returns to his chest. With the odour of her hair and body, a slightly stale smell of breath hovers over him. A little earlier, Sweta seemed asleep. He must have woken her up with his yawn. Before Aditya realises, Sweta pulls her pillow and comes close to him.

"Why aren't you sleeping!"

"I don't know." Aditya says, "I woke up suddenly."

"Why? Are you unwell?"

"No." Aditya keeps quiet for a little while. And then say, "I don't know."

"I know. In worry." Sweta mumbles, "God knows what you're always thinking."

"What's there to think about? Nothing."

"Say that to yourself." Sweta's fingers run through his hair. She says, "Even if you don't say no, I know something has happened. Pritha feels the same too."

"What!"

Sweta is half-asleep. Yawning, she comes as close to him as possible. And says, "You're always tense and worried. What can we say! When everyone is asleep, you walk about, you won't say anything so we don't ask."

Sweta's voice cracks in emotion. Her hand moves from his head to his neck and then clutches his shoulders. Aditya turns to feel the warmth of her heavy bosom. Burying himself in the flesh of her open blouse, he says, "Each person has a hidden world—the world of his personal thoughts. You can't talk loudly about that world. Even if I told you, you wouldn't understand."

"I don't know. You seem to be growing distant even though we are under the same roof."

The dry fields are getting washed in the rain, the earth is muddy and ready for sowing. Before throwing herself open, Sweta's lips touch Aditya's cheek—trying to cover the distance. And then says, "You said you fell asleep that night you returned from Bombay! The durwan told Satya that you had gone for a morning walk as usual. You returned suddenly in a taxi. You came as if someone was chasing you. I came to know of it today."

Aditya stops and asks, "Did Satya tell you?"

"How would I know otherwise?"

"That's true."

Aditya slowly releases the stifled breath. And says in a normal tone, "I didn't tell you because there was reason not to. I'll tell you tomorrow, everyone will come to know tomorrow."

Sweta doesn't reply. Pulling Aditya's face towards herself, she says, "It's raining. You needn't go out today."

Chapter 5

Aditya knew his life wouldn't remain the same. But did he know that it would change him completely—from being agitated at newspaper reports to being news himself, from the monotony of security at home and office, he would enter the warfield, did he know that?

Things start happening fast and unexpectedly, once the letter is printed in the newspaper.

"You haven't done the right thing." Ashok Dutta says over the phone in the morning, "Too much of a risk."

"Why!" Aditya asks. Then, seeing Ashok silent, jokes, "One proof of how great and charitable the police of a democratic state is, how they're taking the law in their own hands to maintain order."

Ashok doesn't reply immediately. he says in a stunned voice, "Don't attack me for being in the police force. I'm your friend as well. Besides, only newspaper letters can't prove anything."

"What are you hinting at?"

"The paper made a scoop of your letter this time—maybe to create a sensation. But, you must realise what it does to you."

"I didn't to it for my personal gain."

Ashok ponders. He says, "I don't know what the police is going to do about your letter. But, there's another danger. Factionalism has deepened among the Naxals. They're attacking each other nastily. It would be dangerous if they try to use you. Be careful."

"Let's see." Aditya stops.

In the meantime, more news pour in.

Pradipta visits him one day. He asks, "Can you remember the appearance of the murdered man properly?"

"Why?"

Pradipta doesn't reply.

Aditya says, "I know nothing more than what I wrote in the letter. I only remember the man was thin and tall. At least it seemed so. Nothing more was visible."

"It seems a coincidence. But unlikely." Pradipta says, "The night Saibal Majumdar was supposed to have been arrested, you witnessed the murder the following dawn. Of course, the police haven't confirmed the arrest. You must have read in the papers, the official report has denied it. On the other hand, rumour is, the man arrested was not Saibal Majumdar at all—a half-wit neurotic. The police released him that same night. Charu Majumdar gave a statement, Saibal Majumdar was killed the night he was arrested."

These are just reports. He has read them in the newspapers. Holding his breath, Aditya says, "I don't know. I would have told you if I knew."

"It's difficult. You could have if you had known Saibal Majumdar in person. Anyway—" Pradipta rises abruptly, "Your letter has created a commotion. It's been referred to the Centre. The police might harrass you. Don't worry. Warn your family and let us know if anything happens."

Kanchan still visits carrying his camera. He's restless to tear up the solemnity of the Wood Street flat and normalise it. He mentions one day, "You're being hotly discussed, Adityada."

"What's there to discuss about me"

"That letter of yours—." He adjusts the camera lens out of habit and continues, "Everybody's saying that writing that is letter not possible without courage. The episode has made you news."

Aditya looks Kanchan straight in the face but hesitantly. He says, "I know. Your Dhruva Nandi had called. He said filmstars spread scandals to get into the limelight. I've set the trend as a writer, he said."

Kanchan is upset.

"I didn't say that, Adityada. I believe nodody would dare to write that letter at a time like this. You were alone— no other witness. It's your lone fight."

Aditya smiles. Looks at sky beyond the balcony. A plane is flying low at a distance. The sound doesn't reach here. Two kites have flying ahead got entangled. Observing all these in a distracted manner, he murmurs, "I don't know.

I don't know if it's a fight at all. Who's the adversary?" He continues, "I don't know how people are interpreting it. How does it help me if I know? I only know the fight was with myself."

Sweta and Pritha are grim. Bachchu is too young to realise. Aditya observes they are no longer in the game of teasing Kanchan. They would have to speak if they look up, so their eyes wander. True, his life is changing.

"So many people are being killed all around." Pritha says suddenly, "One murder only increases the number. What difference would it make if you didn't write that letter?"

"Nothing would change in the world." Aditya smiles solemnly. "But I would feel low."

Pritha keeps silent.

The telephone rings in the middle of the night. Waking up, the buzz seems familiar—it's been ringing long, it would go on forever if the caller can't get in touch with him. Each ring pierces into the darkness.

Getting up, Aditya sees that Sweta is already up. To dissuade her, he says, "You stay here. I'll take it."

"No. I'll take it."

Sweta switches on the light. They both walk out of the bedroom. Pritha is already. She looks into Aditya's eyes. She says in a worried voice, "You wait, I'll take it."

To ease the tension, Aditya says, "Calls would come if there's a phone in the house. Why're you scared?"

A large vehicle is clattering its bonnet down the road. Sweta looks at Aditya as if she can see the colour and shape of the vehicle clearly. Then, looking at the telephone, says, "We have no relative in Calcutta who can expire suddenly. Nobody would stay awake so late to ask for your writing—"

Aditya doesn't reply. He doesn't object. He is quiet to see Pritha picking up the receiver.

"Hello—"

Not even in ten seconds, Pritha scolds, "Wrong number. Please don't disturb us so late in the night."

Pritha hangs up. She looks straight at Aditya.

Swetha looks at her husband and asks her daughter, a little disturbed.

"Wrong number?"

"No, He was asking for Baba. An unknown voice."

Aditya says, "Then why did you say wrong number?"

Pritha doesn't reply immediately. Walking past Aditya and Sweta, she says, "The caller was definitely not your friend."

Returning to the bedroom, Sweta says, "Was it the police?"

"Why should it be the police?" Aditya brushes it off, "Why are you all so scared?"

Sweta switches off the light. The sky is starry, the moonlight gleams too. A bit of it is peeping through the window. Aditya can see half of Sweta's face. The wind is uncertain at one o'clock at night. It hasn't rained for two days. Yet, instead of warming up, the air is cool.

Pulling up the sheet and lying down, she says "We're not scared for ourselves."

It's not just a change from one state of things to another, Aditya feels, life is changing—the roots are being tugged at. At the same time, his sense of security is getting overhauled. So long he has been worrying about Sweta, Pritha, now they're anxious over him. They'll worry even if he tells them not to.

He moves to the bed with no further word. The moonlight dances off the walls to touch his feet. Staring at the feet he is reminded of a funeral procession. That's how men leave the world.

Sweta turns. She lays a hand on Aditya's chest.

"Can I say something?"

"What?"

"There'll be trouble here." Sweta says, "Let's go to Animesh's for a few days. Poona's a nice place. If we stay there for some time, things will cool down here. Then we'll come back."

Aditya knows Sweta's brother Animesh is in Poona. He often calls them up. Sweta too wants to visit him. They haven't been able to make it. He keeps quiet for some time and says, "Want me to run away? That'll show that I'm scared."

"That's the problem with you." Sweta says, "You're adamant."

Before he replies, the telephone starts ringing again. That same ring—continuous, sharp, going on for ages.

This time, Aditya himself makes a dash for it. Picking up the receiver, he sees Pritha has come out of her room.

"Hello."

"Is it Adityababu?"

Faint, a slightly rough voice. As it sounds over a long distance call. Not a familiar one. As Aditya is silent, the voice shouts, "Hello, hello."

"Yes."

"Is it Aditya Ray?"

The caller seems to be in a hurry. Aditya's brow creases. "Who's it?"

"It won't help you to know that. You're Aditya Ray?"

"Yes."

"Listen." The voice becomes clearer, "We've read your letter. What you've written is nothing. The person you saw murdered was Comrade Saibal Majumdar. You knew him—"

The dial tone returns as the line is disconnected. Aditya holds on to the receiver inspite of knowing there's no point. Then he puts it down slowly.

He has been hearing these words for a long time. They are heavy but not sharp. Knocking them will give a metallic sound. But the worry is not on account of that. Aditya tries to make out what the point was to threaten him this way. Had they come forward to ask, he would have explained that there's no point in this. Shouting oneself hoarse and calling someone class enemy doesn't classify a man. If you had matured, you would have realised I don't belong to any class. I'm alone—very lonely. Or I'm a class by myself. Maybe there are a few more like me, I don't know them.

Pritha asks, "Who was it, Baba?"

"A ghost call." Aditya smiles faintly at his daughter's scared face. Sweta is standing, holding on to the curtain. With a lost look. Aditya says, "We seem to have fallen into strange times. We don't trust anyone, don't try to understand. Only wake people up in the middle of the night and frighten them."

"I know who called you."

Pritha grows paler.

Aditya approaches his daughter. He keeps an affectionate hand on her back.

"You, like your friends, know everything."

"You're hedging Baba." Pritha says in a faltering voice, "Do you realise what's happening all around?"

"Don't I!" Aditya tries to calm himself, "Could I go this far if I hedged?"

Sweta says, "I don't understand your riddle. You'll kill yourself, kill us too."

"Ma, what are you saying?"

"Forget it!" Aditya stops the mother and daughter. He says, "The more you brood, the more worried you'll get. Bachchu will wake up. Rather, let's chat. We can't sleep any more—"

Chapter 6

On 23rd August, in the middle of the night, it starts pouring. torrential rain, there is thunder and lightning. The noise is deafening. In the midst of this, the doorbell rings.

Sweta springs up. She tugs at Aditya.

"Do you hear?"

"Yes." Aditya keeps quiet for some time. And then says, "Switch on the lights. I'll see."

Pritha is up too. Aditya hears her voice from outside the room, "Baba, somebody's ringing the bell. Shall I see?"

"No. I'm coming."

Sweta switches on the light. Aditya pulls at his kurta. He rubs his eyes and runs his fingers through his hair. And then goes ahead to open the door.

A few moments. Aditya doesn't take more time than needed to realise who the people are. A little agitated, his lips tremble. And then says, "What's it?"

"Sorry, Mr Ray. You'll have to come with us—"

"Where?"

"You'll know. We have the arrest warrant."

"I see." Aditya doesn't believe in God. Yet, this moment, he prays for some supernatural power. He tries to be bold, "Give me a little time."

As he turns, he sees Sweta run back. Pritha runs to him, after standing in a stupor. She holds on to Aditya, "Baba, you won't go. They'll kill you too."

"Don't be crazy, Pritha." Pulling his daughter inside, Aditya says, "It's not so easy to kill somebody. Why don't you understand, they wouldn't have arrested me if they weren't scared."

Pritha tries to control herself, biting her lips.

Aditya enters the bedroom. He sees Sweta leaning against the wall. Without saying a word, he picks up his trousers, shirt. He goes to the toilet. Returning, he says, "Don't be scared."

Putting the purse and the pen in his pocket, Aditya slips on his sandals. Before going out, he lays a hand on Sweta's shoulder.

"Don't wake up Bachchu. Inform Kanchan. You know what to do."

Sweta looks away. She's trying her best to control her emotions. She mutters faintly, "Come back."

After takes a look at the sleeping Bachchu, Aditya comes out. He sees Pritha move close. No emotions any more. Palting her back lightly, Aditya says, "I'm leaving. Call

Pradipta after I have left. Tell Debu Chowdhury also. Tell them to inform the office."

Aditya doesn't wait any more. He reaches the door and looks back. He can't see Sweta. He tells Pritha, "Be careful."

Automatic lift. It is being held on the floor. Aditya comes down promptly with the four policemen. He doesn't look around. Moving towards the police van waiting at the gate in the rain, he wonders whether this is that same van, the one that had gone from the street to the darkness of the Maidan—